From Garden to Table

Joan Fielden
Stan Larke

From Garden
to Table

A Complete Guide to Vegetable
Growing and Cooking

Drawings by Margarete Kaufhold

McClelland and Stewart

© McClelland and Stewart, 1976

All rights reserved

ISBN: 0-7710-4790-8 (hardcover)

0-7710-4789-4 (paperback)

The Canadian Publishers
McClelland and Stewart Limited
25 Hollinger Road, Toronto M4B 3G2

Design by Michael van Elsen

Printed and bound in Canada

Contents

Growing

Cooking

Grow and Cook

Grow and Cook

continued

Final Touches

Growing

Those people who are serious about gardening will find a way to grow all or at least some of their own fresh vegetables no matter what their life-style or surroundings. Whether they choose planter boxes on an apartment balcony, a few precious feet of urban property, or a spacious country lot, the same basic desire to reap from the soil prevails. Even where meagre space permits the growing of only one or two tomato plants, or one cabbage, or a simple flowerpot of parsley, one gains satisfaction from growing one's own food. After all, is anything more delicious than fresh picked vegetables from the garden?

Fortunate indeed are those who have enough space in which to grow their entire fresh vegetable requirements. In the cases where space is limited, the gardener can be consoled by the fact that science and the horticulture industry are doing everything to derive the most benefit from the tiniest amount of soil — almost anywhere.

For gardeners with a reasonable amount of outdoor space, the familiar bulk raw materials, such as manure, peat moss, garden compost, leafmold and all the other standard soil additives and improvers, are available in large quantities. Window-boxes or balcony planters require only the purchase of a plastic bag of soil. All the necessary ingredients are contained in these bags in exactly the right proportions, sterilized, disinfected, and even deodorized. It is now practical to grow vegetables in mixtures of organic, inorganic, and synthetic materials such as "peatlite," a mixture of peat moss and vermiculite, which only needs to be watered and fertilized in order to support plant growth.

The Basic Facts

THE PROPER USE OF AVAILABLE SPACE

The home vegetable garden will certainly help stretch the family food dollars. The cost of the average vegetable patch, which usually measures 30 x 100 feet, including seeds, fertilizers, dusts and sprays, will likely run below $20.

If the produce from the garden is consumed during the growing season, the value of the vegetables will be about $100. If the harvest, or some of it, is stored and consumed during the winter, the value of the vegetables will increase to about $130. During the bountiful months of August and September, when supply is often in excess of demand, it may be cheaper to buy vegetables and store the homegrown harvest for the winter when prices are higher.

SOW THE CROP THAT SUITS THE SPACE

If your garden plot is small, avoid the vegetables that require large amounts of space, such as cucumbers, melons, potatoes, and squash. Instead, plant vegetables that respond to intensive cultivation. Plan ahead for a garden that can support a succession of plantings. After harvesting the early crops of lettuce, radishes, and spinach, use the same space for planting late beets, cabbage, or carrots. Make several seedings of such crops as radishes, spinach, lettuce, peas, and beans, which are edible for only a short period of time. In the case of sweet corn, plant several varieties at the same time.

In areas where the growing season is short, it might be best to cut down to two sowings of peas and beans. A second seeding of corn about fourteen days after the first is also advisable in areas with a shorter growing season.

Vegetables that mature fast, such as lettuce, radishes and spinach, can be planted between rows of crops like eggplant and tomatoes that require wide spacing through the whole growing season. It is common to harvest as many as three crops of green onions, radishes, spinach, and leaf lettuce while slower-growing vegetables are producing their single annual crop.

SELECTING THE LOCATION

Since most vegetable gardens need at least six hours of sunlight in the warm part of the day, choose a sunny location. Avoid shaded areas near buildings or under shrubs and trees. The roots of trees and bushes will compete for the moisture and plant food in the soil.

The Ideal Soil

Vegetables grow best in deep, sandy loam containing sand, clay, and organic matter in reasonable balance. Gravelly loams and clay loams are also good. The deeper the layer of surface soil — or topsoil — the better the crops. Sandy loam and gravelly loam are easy to work and are classed as early soils as they warm up quickly in the spring; however, they also lose moisture badly during the dry weather. Clay loam is more difficult to work and must be handled carefully. Digging this kind of soil when it is wet or too dry causes lumpiness or hard clods that make preparation of a fine-textured seed bed difficult.

In almost every case the gardener will discover that his soil requires some improving and conditioning in order to sustain sturdy, healthy crops.

SOIL CONDITIONERS

Generally speaking, sandy soils or gravelly soils require one or more applications of organic matter to improve their moisture-holding capacity. This matter should be worked into the top six inches of soil. Denser soils, such as clay, also require one or more thorough applications of organic matter not only to help hold moisture, but also to help open the dense soil particles and allow the penetration of moisture and air. In addition dense soils require such inorganic and synthetic materials as sharp sand, baked brick chips, perlite and baked-clay granules to make a coarse texture which allows for better drainage of excess water.

What are organic materials? The most popular organic matter in use by home gardeners is peat moss, followed in popularity by well-rotted barnyard manure, garden compost, chopped straw, leafmold, sawdust, and woodchips.

Peat moss is well known for its capacity to retain moisture in the amount of seven times its own weight. It is usually available in handy bales of various sizes and weights to meet the individual gardener's needs.

Well-rotted manure is an excellent soil conditioner, although it should not be considered as a source of complete plant food — commercial fertilizers should also be applied. In addition to supplying some plant food, manure helps to improve the moisture-holding capacity of the soil, allows the penetration of air and water, and provides a home for vital soil bacteria and micro-organisms. The plant food content of manure varies a great deal, depending on the animal which produced the manure and the nature of the animal's diet. Sheep and poultry manures are richer in plant food constituents than pig, horse, and cow manures. Pig manure, although it may be of high quality, is not often used. Cow manure, because of its greater bulk and availability, is the most widely used. Take special care to be certain that all manure is either fully composted or well rotted before it is incorporated into the garden soil. Non-rotted manures contain strong acids and countless weed seeds which can only result in needless trouble.

For use in balcony or indoor gardening, as well as in the garden, composted and deodorized manures are available in easy-to-handle sealed containers. Where manure is difficult to obtain and where the bagged composted manures are not practical, the compost pile becomes essential. Compost, or artificial manure, is prepared by the process of decomposition of all waste vegetable matter on your property including grass clippings, leaves, vegetable peelings, garden refuse, and even domestic garbage. If it is organic in structure, it can be composted, although fibrous materials, such as wood and paper, require a very long time to break down. The miracle of decomposition is accomplished by nature's hardest workers, the insects and bacteria that act as the earth's janitors. When nature renders vegetable matter useless for any other purpose, the busy decomposers consume it, pass it through their digestive systems and return it to the soil as priceless humus to support the next step in the ecological cycle. After hundreds of years of this continuing natural process perhaps an inch of priceless topsoil will be produced.

In order for the gardener to hasten decomposition, a small amount of nitrogenous fertilizer may be applied to each six- or eight-inch layer of green waste as it goes on the pile. Industry has also produced a product which speeds up decomposition and helps keep down odours. Keep the pile of layers of green matter moistened, and in three to six months, if the pile has been turned over once or twice, the organic compost should be ready to be applied to the garden soil.

None of the above-mentioned organic materials should be considered to be the source of complete plant food (or fertilizer) for the garden. A commercial fertilizer should also be applied if the soil is to be rich enough to provide the heavy nourishment demands of vegetables. Because the subject of fertilizers is so vast and complex, you should ask for advice from a local authority. Many fertilizer manufacturers have now produced a product-line that is suited specifically for vegetables, and the chances are that one of these will be available in the stores in your district. Whatever fertilizer is used, the directions for application printed on the container must be followed for satisfactory results.

THE AMOUNT OF SOIL CONDITIONERS AND FERTILIZER NEEDED

As to how much of the organic material, and/or inert and synthetic conditioners to use, this is a decision the individual must make on the basis of his specific needs. Just remember that since it is not likely you will "over-supply" the garden with organic matter, be generous with it on all types of soils. Two or three inches spread over the entire surface of the garden would not be amiss. The amount of sand and other coarse conditioners needed will depend on how much it takes to make your soil friable and easy to work. Experiment on a small section, adding and mixing, until the soil has the right texture; then add the same proportions to the rest of the garden. The fertilizer, which is added at the same time as the conditioners, should be applied only at the rates stated on the container.

Soil conditioners and fertilizers are applied over the entire garden area and then forked, spaded, ploughed, or tilled to a depth of at least six to eight inches. Use power tilling equipment where practical to keep the backache out of this important phase of vegetable gardening. From here on it's all downhill.

SEEDBED PREPARATION

Even after the soil is well conditioned, the seedbed must be prepared afresh each year. The nourishment and organic matter will have been used by the previous year's crop and will have to be replaced. The soil for seeds must be level, fine-textured, and free of lumpy and fibrous matter.

The time to begin preparing the seedbed is in the fall, if possible, or in the spring as soon as the ground is dry enough to be worked. Spread organic matter over the soil, and then plough, till, or spade the soil and organic matter thoroughly.

Where the soil is already well supplied with humus (organic matter), 50 pounds of manure or compost per 100 square feet of soil will suffice. On poorer soils, double the amount of manure or compost. Commercial fertilizer is added after the organic matter has been worked well into the soil six to eight inches deep. Work the soil well, either by hand or with power equipment, making sure that all the organic matter is thoroughly incorporated into the top layer. All existing sod should be turned under and completely covered. Where couch, twitch, or quack grass is present, shake out all the roots with a digging fork. Next comes the application of commercial fertilizer. Scatter it over the surface according to the directions on the container. Work in the fertilizer with a rake or harrow. Then thoroughly pulverize and rake the surface of the garden as smooth as possible in order to obtain a uniform stand of plants from both seeds and transplants.

The Garden Layout

It is at this point that all your advance planning begins to pay off. The vegetable garden that is laid out properly will produce much more bountifully than the poorly planned one. Plan the garden so that the tall-growing plants, such as corn, staked tomatoes, and pole beans, will be at the north side where they will not cast shade on smaller plants. Where there is a slope involved, run the rows across the slope to prevent water run-off and soil erosion.

To allow for proper cultivation of perennial vegetables (those that stay year after year) such as asparagus and rhubarb, place them on the edge of the garden about three feet from the grass or fence line.

Plant the vine crops (melons, squash, cucumber, etc.) in the centre of the garden and the other crops at each side, with two rows of the early vegetables along the edges of the vine crops. The early vegetables will be matured and harvested by the time the vine crops start spreading out. If possible, rotate the different plantings from year to year, trying not to have the same crops on the same ground all the time. It is especially important that cabbage and turnip be given a fresh place in the garden each year in order to prevent a build-up of soil-borne pests. Onions and vine crops can stay in the same locations each year.

WHICH VARIETIES OF VEGETABLES TO GROW

The question of which vegetables to grow is answered best by an honest appraisal of what vegetables your family prefers. Obviously, there is no point in taking up garden space growing vegetable marrow if none of the family will eat it.

When you have decided which vegetables you are going to grow, you must then select the proper varieties for your local area. Not all varieties of all vegetables will grow under all climatic conditions. Some varieties need a lot of very hot weather, while others thrive in cool temperatures either very early or very late in the season.

Vegetables come in three categories: frost-hardy, semi-frost-hardy, and frost-tender. The term "frost-hardy" does not mean that these vegetables will not freeze, but that they are hardy enough to resist a few degrees of frost. The following are considered frost-hardy: asparagus, broccoli, Brussels sprouts, cabbage, Chinese cabbage, cress, kohlrabi, leaf lettuce, onion and related crops, parsley, radish, rhubarb, peas, spinach, turnip, kale, and parsnip. These crops are sown well in advance of the frost-tender types because they require cool growing weather. Crops such as cauliflower, radish, spinach, and turnip do not grow well in the hottest part of the summer.

Semi-frost-hardy vegetables can withstand a little frost but not so much as the frost-hardy types. Some of the semi-frost-hardy types of vegetables do not germinate quickly in cold soil and are therefore sown almost as early in the season as the frost-hardy types. There is generally a long waiting period before these crops emerge above soil level. The following are considered semi-frost-hardy: beets, carrots, cauliflower, celery, chard, endive, head lettuce, herbs, and potato. Also the tomato when seeded outside. Celery is more susceptible to frost damage in the spring than in the fall. Leaf lettuce will develop better in cooler, wetter conditions than will head lettuce. The above ground parts of corn and potatoes may sometimes be killed by frost, but if the soil is fertile and enough energy remains in the seed, they will probably return to vigorous growth and produce an excellent but later crop.

Frost-tender vegetables are those that cannot withstand any frost at all. Included in this group are beans, cucumbers, eggplants, muskmelons, okra, peppers, pumpkins, squash, tomatoes and watermelons.

A WORD ABOUT SEEDS

Don't be stingy or bargain-conscious at seed buying time. Compared with the value of the vegetables harvested, the cost of seeds is a pittance. Buy the best seeds available.

Sowing the Seeds Outdoors

The procedure for sowing seeds directly into the garden will be described in detail as each individual vegetable is discussed throughout the book. It should be noted that one of the most important phases of vegetable gardening is "thinning" vegetable seedlings to the proper spacing. When vegetable plants are allowed to grow too close together, they crowd each other out, stunt and distort the size and shape of the vegetables (if they even produce vegetables), and generally reduce the quantity and quality of the crop. On the other hand, planting the vegetables too far apart is just a waste of valuable garden space.

Starting the Seeds Indoors

An ever-growing number of home gardeners prefer to sow vegetable seeds indoors, thin the seedlings, and then transplant healthy, sturdy young plants into the garden without fear of frost or failure.

Apartment and window-box gardeners should be heartened with the knowledge that many nurseries and garden centres now sell single vegetable plants pre-started in their own individual peat pots which need only be placed to the rim in soil with almost guaranteed results.

THE MODERN WAY

Before getting down to the final nitty-gritty of how to sow the seeds indoors, it should be stated that modern science has now brought this phase of gardening out of the dark ages and into our modern world. Except for greatly experienced gardeners, I recommend forgetting all the old methods and looking at indoor seed-sowing in the modern way.

It is no longer necessary to mix your own seedling soils and then purify them to get rid of diseases, insects, and unwanted seeds. Because such a small quantity of soil for seeds is required, it is practical to buy prepared soils in which to start the seeds for the home garden. With these prepared soils there is no fuss, no muss, no bother. Just ask your local dealer for the proper mixture for starting seeds.

There is a vast variety of seed-starting containers (which entirely replace the need for seed pans and flats), many of which are actually miniature greenhouses. In almost every case, these seedling containers come with detailed instructions for sowing and growing.

It has also become quite acceptable to sow the single seeds of larger vegetables in containers that are made of a mixture of compressed peat moss and wood fiber. These containers, often called peat pots or jiffy pots, can be placed in the vegetable garden as is, once the plant has become well-rooted indoors. Certain vegetable crops that were, until the development of the peat pot, considered impractical to start indoors because of transplanting difficulties (muskmelon, cucumber, squash, etc.) can now be safely handled because the roots remain undisturbed at transplanting time. Once planted the peat pots soon dissolve in outdoor acid and neutral soils.

When sowing seeds in peat pots, the seed is gently pressed into soil or sowing medium and barely covered. Water lightly. Unless instructions on the container state otherwise, the moist and seeded pots must be shaded. A sheet of newspaper will provide the necessary shade and will also keep the moisture in.

When the seedlings emerge, remove the shading, and place the containers in strong light to develop short, sturdy plants.

Before placing the seedlings in the garden, the plants should be exposed to outdoor conditions gradually. (See page 18 for "hardening-off" instructions.)

THE OLD-FASHIONED WAY

If it just doesn't suit your nature to abandon the methods your grandfather used when preparing transplants, all well and good. In that case, your sterilized soil mixture should consist of seven parts loam, three parts peat moss, and two parts sand. Add about two ounces of superphosphate, or complete fertilizer, to each bushel of mixture. Sift the soil mixture through a half-inch sieve to remove rough and lumpy materials and dampen it before seeding.

Sow each kind of seed in a different container to make transplanting more convenient. Six-inch seed pans, or five-inch flower pots will be plenty large enough to start all the seedlings of each vegetable needed for the average garden.

Pack the soil mixture fairly firmly in the containers, sow the seeds, and then cover lightly with more of the soil mixture. The depth of planting depends on the size of the seed. The correct depth is twice the diameter of the seed. Check to see that all soil is level when you cover the seeds, or some may be deeper than others and fail to germinate.

Water with a fine spray to avoid uncovering the little seeds. An alternative method of watering at this stage is to place the pot two-thirds of its depth in water and keep it there until the soil surface darkens; then remove and allow it to drain. Glass or plastic should then be placed over the container to conserve moisture and lessen the need for further waterings. Shade the seeded pots and pans from direct sunlight until the first seedlings appear; then remove the cover for full exposure to the light. When exposed to full light, the tiny plants will grow squat and strong. In poor light they tend to become weak and spindly as they reach upward to catch the vital sunshine.

WHEN TO TRANSFER TO FLATS

Whether you are using modern methods of indoor seeding, or following the old-fashioned way, the day will come when seedlings must be removed from their containers and replanted at proper spacings in larger containers, usually called flats, where they will grow until time to be placed outdoors. When using certain types of modern seed starters the seedlings do not have to be picked out, rather they stay where they are from seeding time until transplanted outdoors. This feature will be clearly marked on the container's instructions. Starting the very large seeds of such vegetables as squash, pumpkin and cucumber, in individual peat pots is also a one-step planting. These seedlings stay in the same containers even after being placed in the garden.

Transfer the seedlings into flats after they have developed their first three or four leaves. Use the same mixture of soil in the flats as in the seedling pots, pans, and containers, and space the transplants about two inches apart in straight rows. Puncture a drill-hole in the levelled soil surface using your finger, a pencil, or a sharpened peg. Then insert one seedling to a hole and gently firm the soil around the roots. To keep them short and sturdy, place the seedlings in a well-lit location. Keep the soil evenly moist, and, to reduce damping-off disease, water early in the day so that the foliage is dry by nightfall.

DAMPING-OFF DISEASE

One of the biggest headaches in raising seedlings indoors comes from a fungus that is present in most moist soils called "damping-off." This disease causes the seedlings to rot at the base where they contact the soil and to topple over. In some cases, the seedlings fail to emerge.

There are two positive methods of controlling damping-off disease. Fumigation of the soil is the oldest remedial action. Get a bottle of commercial Formalin from a druggist or feed store. The Formalin will contain 37 per cent formaldehyde. To treat one bushel of soil, put two tablespoons of Formalin in a cup and fill the cup with water. Sprinkle this mixture over the soil and mix well. To make sure that the fumes penetrate all the soil, cover the container with layers of damp paper or plastic sheeting for 48 hours. When you take the cover off and the smell disappears, the soil will be ready for the delicate seeds. Caution is urged in this process. It is wise to mix the Formalin in the garage with the door open, or mix it outside. The fumes are unpleasant and will irritate the eyes and nose.

The second and simpler way of controlling damping-off is by means of chemicals that are compounded just for this purpose. They are prepared under a large number of trade names. If you ask for a product to control damping-off, you'll be sold the proper item.

WHAT IS A FLAT?

The term "flat" is used to describe the containers into which the tiny seedlings are placed to complete their growth before being transplanted outdoors. A flat can be in any size wooden berry box, a shallow fruit box, a fish box, or any container that will hold at least three inches of soil and allow excess water to drain away. The most satisfactory flat is about 12-1/2 x 22 inches, with sides 3 inches deep. To make such a flat, use wood 5/8-inch thick and 12 inches long for the ends, and 1/4-inch thick, 22 inches long, and 3 inches wide for the sides and bottom. Leave a little space between the bottom pieces to permit drainage. Using flats of standard size permits them to be shifted and readily replaced by others. When they are not in use, store them in a dry place and they will give years of service.

HARDENING OFF TRANSPLANTS

Many transplants are lost every year because the gardener simply took his flats out of doors and immediately transferred them to the garden. It must be remembered that all young transplants are extremely tender and have never experienced anything but the almost perfect growing environment indoors. No one should expect them to survive the tremendous shock of a sudden change of climatic conditions. It would be similar to shipping a human being in a bathing suit from a sandy beach in the sunny south directly to an Eskimo igloo in the far north—the shock would be too much.

Make the change from indoor living to outdoors a gradual thing. Move the flats outdoors on a dull, cloudy day and place them in a sheltered spot where wind won't harm them. Leave them for one hour the first day. Next day increase the time to about two hours, and so on, until the plants have made a gradual adjustment to the cooler, windy, sometimes parching outdoors. When the stems have become hardened and less watery, they should be strong enough to withstand the exodus to the garden. Your gentle care and kind attention does not end there. The young plants will still require protection from wind and sun. A plant must have a lot of stamina to survive what is called "transplanting shock." A board on edge, or a wooden shingle placed beside each plant will provide a wind break and, if put on the south side, will also shade out the searing rays of the sun until the plant is strong enough to withstand the stresses on its own.

HOW TO TRANSPLANT

Several hours before transplanting, water the plants thoroughly and transplant them during dull weather or in the evening when the soil is moist. Use stocky, healthy plants with a good root system. Cabbage should have leaves from four to six inches long; tomato plants should be eight to ten inches high.

When individual seeds or transplants have been grown in peat pots, there is no need to remove the pot when settling the plants in the garden. Simply place the potted plant in a hole deep enough to cover the rim of the peat pot, gently firm the soil around it, and then water. With this method there is little or no setback to the plants.

When transplanting from such containers as berry boxes, cut the box at the four corners and remove the plants without disturbing the soil. When transplanting from a pot, turn the pot bottom up in the hand and loosen the earth containing the plant by tapping the rim on something solid. When transplanting from a flat, cut the soil to the bottom of the flat in squares, leaving a block of soil with the plant in the centre.

Make the holes in the garden large enough to receive the transplants and at the proper distances apart. Place the plants carefully in the holes without disturbing the ball of earth around the roots. Fill in the soil and press it firmly but gently around the plant. In very dry soil, water once right after transplanting to soak the soil thoroughly and settle it around the plants. Tomato plants that are shorter than ten inches should be placed in a shallow trench with six inches of the plant showing above ground level. After they become established with good strong roots, draw earth in around them using water to puddle the soil into direct contact with the roots. When the plants are set, press the soil firmly around them, taking care not to squash the stem at ground level.

General Care of the Vegetable Patch

Now that the soil has been prepared, the garden laid out properly, and the transplants are in and the seeds have been sown, we cannot walk away and wait for the harvest to come along all by itself. The entire area will need to be watered at least once a week (more often in very hot weather) especially when there is no rain. Weeds will have to be removed because they rob vegetables of vital moisture and plant food. Finally, you must be constantly alert to the ever-possible insect infestation or disease infection and be prepared to take appropriate measures.

VEGETABLE GARDEN CHEMICALS

In the hands of irresponsible or uninformed people, who are apt to misuse them, chemicals are terribly dangerous. Informed gardeners, however, are fully aware that some of the most brilliant minds in horticultural, agricultural, chemical, and environmental sciences have given their approval to the use of chemicals and have laid down the rules and regulations. Government bodies test and retest all chemicals under the most rigorous conditions imaginable and either approve, restrict, or deny their use. Long before they ever arrive in the stores for the public's use, all chemicals have been prepared under strict regulations. In a word, garden chemicals are safe when applied according to the directions on the containers.

For those who are prepared to accept the responsibility of the proper handling of chemicals, the following list will indicate some of the general uses for which they have been prepared, as related to vegetable gardening:

ridding the soil of unwanted grasses,
preventing the germination of weed seeds,
destroying soil-borne insects both visible and microscopic,
destroying flying, crawling and sucking insects,
preventing and controlling plant diseases,
preventing the ravages of rodents,
assisting in the rapid decomposition of vegetable waste,
improving the supply of vital food elements in the soil as fertilizer.

Whenever the gardener has a need for assistance in doing any of the above tasks, he will find the right product on the market bearing complete application instructions.

CULTIVATING

As soon as the rows of young seedlings emerge, or immediately after the transplants are set out, start hoeing. Kill the weeds when they are small, before they can use up much plant food and moisture. Hoeing during bright sunshine will destroy the weeds completely. However, large weeds should be pulled from the crop row only when the soil is moist; otherwise the vegetable plant roots may be damaged when exposed to sun and wind in dry soil.

For a healthy crop, cultivate the ground once a week to a depth of one or two inches. As the plants increase in size and cover more and more of the earth, hoe less of the space between the rows, and hoe shallower to avoid injuring the roots.

MULCHING

The amount of work involved in weeding the vegetable garden can be greatly reduced by mulching the rows. Most common mulching materials include grass clippings, hay or straw, sawdust, woodchips, sometimes even corn cobs. Where the gardener has access to a supply of oat hulls (or the hulls of other grains) from such places as flour mills, grain elevators, and distillers, this material also makes an excellent mulch.

When a covering of mulch is properly applied to the vegetable garden, three important things occur: weeds cannot penetrate the mulch and are therefore eradicated; soil moisture will not evaporate as rapidly and the possibility of drought is almost eliminated; and the soil temperature is kept at a cooler, healthier level for plant growth. Remember that a covering of mulch material leaves only the desirable plants while all others are buried and smothered.

It has become popular to mulch the vegetable garden with strips of black polyethylene plastic. The plastic is spread over the entire bed area and held in place with stones, boards, or pegs. When transplanting, a small hole is poked through the plastic sheet, and the plant is inserted through it into the soil. In cases where seeds are sown into the garden soil outdoors, plastic sheets are spread between the rows covering the full width from one row of plants to the next over every possible inch of soil surface.

Except in the cases of plastic mulches, the mulch material can be turned into the soil after harvest in the fall to increase the organic matter in the vegetable patch.

PLANTING AND HARVEST DATES

Suggested sowing and harvesting dates, both indoors and outdoors, are subject to change according to frost conditions in local areas. This also applies to suggested transplanting dates.

Vegetable Storage

When it is not practical to freeze, pickle, or preserve, other storage facilities must be provided, often calling for special conditions.

Beans and peas should be stored in a cool, dry location, an attic, a porch, or an unheated room. They should be kept in polyethylene bags or glass jars after shelling. Beets, carrots, parsnips, cabbage, and onions require a storage temperature as close as possible to 0° Celsius and an average level of humidity. Potatoes need a constant storage temperature of 5° Celsius, since spoilage will occur at a lower temperature.

VARIATIONS

Beets, parsnips, rutabagas, salsify, and turnips will also store well in damp soil, sprinkled with water as required. Root vegetables, winter squash, cabbage, peas, onions, apples, and hard pears can be stored in shallow crates in a cool, well-ventilated corner of the cellar or outdoor storage cellar or pit. Cabbage, cucumbers, string beans, and turnips lend themselves well to brining or krauting. Corn on the cob dries well.

Cooking

Vegetables are among the best sources of minerals and vitamins. Leaves, stems, roots, and seeds supply carbohydrate in the form of starches, while peas and beans provide protein. Human digestive organs receive essential cellulose from plant's cell walls, thereby enhancing the digestive function. In order to be sure that all the essential nutrients in vegetables do not go to waste, good care and wise cooking are vital.

Whether you are selecting from a store shelf or your own garden, there are a few things to keep in mind about your fresh produce. Be sure your vegetables are firm or crisp and without bruises or blemishes. Clean them as soon as possible and place them in the refrigerator in the crisper or in closed bags. Vegetables that are not suited for the refrigerator, such as onions or potatoes, should be kept in a cool, dry, but ventilated storage area, on wire racks if possible. Try to select vegetables that are in season, when their nutritional value is highest. Maintain the most food value by preparing vegetables at the moment you want to cook them, never in advance.

The art of vegetable cookery is too often neglected or ignored. Vegetables are either overcooked or served with little or no imagination, yet vegetable cookery should not be dull. In our bountiful country there is no excuse for vegetables not to shine. By using choice, tender, young vegetables, good butter, margarine or oil, fine seasonings and care, tasty dishes are virtually guaranteed.

Methods of Cooking Vegetables

BAKING
Cooking in dry heat in the oven.

BOILING
Cooking by immersing the vegetables in a pan of liquid, which must be kept boiling gently—all the time.

BRAISING

Vegetables are placed with a little liquid in a covered vessel, and cooked slowly in the oven or on top of the stove.

CASSEROLE

Cooking slowly in the oven in a covered casserole dish.

FRYING

Often compared to braising. Cooking in a little hot fat in an open pan. Deep frying is cooking by immersion in hot fat, in a deep pan.

OVEN COOKING IN BAGS

Place prepared vegetables in oven bag with two to four tablespoons of water and season to taste. Seal bag as per instructions and bake to desired tenderness.

PRESSURE COOKING

Cooking at a higher temperature than usual under pressure, so that food is cooked much more quickly.

ROASTING

Cooking with a little fat in a hot oven. Fat is poured from the baking pan over the vegetables from time to time, using a long-handled spoon (basting).

SAUTÉEING

Frying in a little fat briefly. Food should be stirred.

SIMMERING

The rate of cooking used for stews—just below boiling point—so that the liquid bubbles gently at the side of the pan.

STEAMING

Cooking either in a steamer over a pan of boiling water, or in a basin standing in (but not covered by) boiling water.

STIR FRYING

This is similar in a sense to sautéeing. The point of stir frying is to keep the food moving constantly so that all parts of the food come in contact with the hottest part of the pan and cook quickly and evenly. This is best done by quickly and repeatedly sliding a spoon or spatula down between the food and the pan and turning the food over on itself with a digging and tossing motion. A wok is the best cooking vessel for stir frying because the sloping sides and rounded bottom help keep the food in motion.

STEWING

Cooking slowly until the food is tender in just enough liquid to cover. The liquid, which is served with the food, should be rich. Stews may be cooked in covered saucepans or casseroles, either on the top of the stove or in the oven—but always at a low temperature.

BOILING

When boiling vegetables, they should be placed in a *small* quantity of boiling salted water. In the case of a large quantity of vegetables, such as cabbage, water should be added slowly rather than all at once to keep the liquid simmering.

Cover the pot and serve the vegetables as soon as they are tender. Overcooking and keeping vegetables hot, even for a short time, will cause a loss of vitamins. When cooking root vegetables, particularly potatoes, simmering, rather than boiling rapidly, is best.

Some basic rules to follow are:

1. Prepare vegetables *just* before cooking.
2. Start cooking in *boiling* water.
3. Use a *small quantity* of water.
4. Adjust heat to keep water boiling *gently*.
5. Cook, covered, only until *tender-crisp*.
6. Season and serve as *soon* as cooked.

PRESSURE COOKING

The importance of cooking vegetables correctly, so that they lose as little as possible of their vitamins and minerals, has been stressed more and more during recent years. Today the accepted way to cook vegetables is to put them into the smallest quantity of water, in a covered container, and cook them for the shortest possible time to desired doneness. In this way they retain not only their vitamin and mineral content but their colour and flavour. A pressure cooker meets these conditions and cooks vegetables to perfection.

When using a pressure cooker, there are some important points to keep in mind.

1. Remember that every minute of pressure cooking time is equivalent to many minutes in an ordinary saucepan, so *time the cooking accurately.*
2. See that the pieces of vegetable are much the same size. If care is not taken, smaller pieces will be badly overcooked by the time the larger pieces are ready.
3. When cooking is completed, pressure should be lowered immediately by putting the cooker under the cold water tap for 10 to 15 seconds. The exception to this rule is when cooking potatoes—they will be more "floury" if pressure is allowed to drop gradually.
4. Since only a small quantity of water is used in pressure cooking vegetables, use less salt or no salt.
5. Unless vegetables are being cooked as part of a meat dish—such as braised or stewed dishes—they will be better if put on a rack inside the pressure cooker.

Times at 15 pound pressure

While the times for pressure cooking the various vegetables are given as accurately as possible, they might vary when larger vegetables are used. Older vegetables will naturally take a little longer to cook.

ARTICHOKES (Globe) 10 minutes.
ARTICHOKES (Jerusalem) 10 minutes.
AUBERGINE or EGGPLANT 3 minutes (stuffed, 4 minutes).
BEANS (Broad) 3 minutes.
BEANS (Haricot) 30 minutes (after soaking).
BEANS (Runner) 2 minutes.
BEETS 10 - 25 minutes.
BRUSSELS SPROUTS 2 minutes.
CABBAGE 2 - 3 minutes.
CARROTS 3 - 8 minutes.
CAULIFLOWER 2 - 5 minutes.
CELERY 3 minutes.

CHICORY 3 minutes.
CORN ON THE COB 4 minutes.
LEEKS 3 minutes.
MUSHROOMS 2 - 3 minutes.
ONIONS 6 minutes.
PEAS (Fresh) 1/2 - 1-1/2 minutes.
PEAS (Dried or split) 15 minutes.
PEPPERS (Red or green, stuffed) 3 - 4 minutes.
POTATOES 8 - 15 minutes.
SALSIFY 10 minutes.
SPINACH 1 minute.
TURNIP (or RUTABAGA) 3 - 8 minutes.
VEGETABLE MARROW 2 minutes.

Note: Cooking times of 3 minutes and under are not usually practical.

How to Freeze Vegetables

BASIC METHOD

Freeze only garden-fresh, clean, tender vegetables.

To heat: Boil one gallon or more water in a large kettle keeping the heat high at all times. Add the vegetables at the rate of one pound per gallon of water, then cover and start timing. Give the thickest pieces the longest time indicated below.

To chill: Plunge the vegetables into iced water until cold. Drain before packing.

To pack: Pack the vegetables in paper cartons with paper or plastic lids, all-plastic containers, or foil cartons. Or use folding cartons with liners, or straight-sided glass jars. Seal if necessary, and mark with date and contents before placing in the freezer. Frozen vegetables under proper care will keep up to one year, but don't forget that the longer they are frozen the more loss of flavour occurs.

Specific examples:

ASPARAGUS. Wash and break off tough ends. Sort into narrow, medium, and thick stalks. Cut into two-inch pieces or leave as spears. Heat two to four minutes, then chill, drain and pack.

GREEN BEANS. Wash and remove ends. Cut into lengthwise strips or one-inch to two-inch pieces. Heat for three minutes. Chill quickly in iced water; drain well and pack.

GREEN LIMAS. Shell and sort according to size, discarding any overmature white beans. Heat two to four minutes, then chill, drain, and pack.

BROCCOLI. Use compact dark-green heads. Wash, trim, and peel stalks if desired. Cut lengthwise leaving one-and-a-half-inch heads. Heat for three minutes. Then chill, drain, and pack.

BRUSSELS SPROUTS. Trim and remove the coarse outer leaves. Wash thoroughly. Sort for size. Heat three to five minutes, according to size. Chill, drain, and pack tightly together.

CORN ON THE COB. Use tender young ears. Husk, wash, and sort ears according to size. Heat small ears seven minutes, medium nine minutes, large eleven minutes. Chill and then either pack or wrap.

WHOLE-KERNEL CORN. Use young tender corn. Husk and wash. Heat four minutes and chill thoroughly. Cut off the kernels without cutting into the cob. Pack tightly in the containers.

GREEN PEPPERS. Wash, and remove stems and seeds. Cut as desired and freeze raw. Or heat halves for three minutes, slices for two minutes. Chill and drain. Peppers should be frozen raw if they are to be stuffed.

MUSHROOMS. Sort for size, wash and trim the ends. Slice mushrooms if larger than one inch. Place in one pint of water with one teaspoon of lemon juice, for five minutes. Drain. Heat whole mushrooms five minutes, slices only three and a half minutes and then chill.

PEAS. Shell, discard the immature or tough peas. Heat one and a half minutes. Chill, drain, and pack. Or freeze on tray, then place in containers for loose pack.

SPINACH. Wash, remove tough stems and older leaves. Heat one and a half to two minutes. Chill, drain thoroughly, and chop if desired.

Vegetables that are considered practical for freezing include the following:

Asparagus	Cauliflower	Potatoes
Beans	Corn	Rhubarb
Broccoli	Mushrooms	Spinach
Brussels sprouts	Parsnip	Turnips
Carrots	Peppers	

Grow and Cook

Climatic conditions will not allow all those who read this book to grow all vegetables. For example, the artichoke requires fairly warm and moist conditions in which to thrive. As a consumer, be content to purchase some vegetables at a neighbourhood store and prepare them for the table using the methods described.

Globe Artichokes

Globe or French artichokes are leafy vegetables that grow on plants resembling thistles. They have a delicately nutty flavour. Although they are low in calories by themselves, they are also the best of excuses for indulging in such high-calorie treats as melted butter, hollandaise sauce, and mayonnaise.

Growing Artichokes

Artichokes do not grow in northern climates.

Cooking Artichokes

1 artichoke (3 inches in diameter) = 33 calories

BASIC PREPARATION

Artichoke quality depends on freshness. Pick them heavy, compact, with fleshy, closely-clinging, crisp leaves and fresh green stems. In winter months, artichokes may have tinges of brown caused by a touch of frost. This is not harmful; indeed, frost is said to tenderize the leaves.

　　Since artichokes discolour quickly after cutting, dip them in lemon juice or vinegar and water until ready to cook.

To cook whole

Wash and drain. Cut off the artichoke stem to a one-inch or half-inch stub. Discard any misshapen leaves. Snip off the thorny tip of each leaf. Cook artichokes in boiling salted water until tender, 35-40 minutes.

To cook hearts

Slice off the stem and remove tough outer leaves. Trim the base smoothly with a sharp knife and cut off pointed tips of the inner leaves.

Scoop out the choke with a small spoon. Cut the heart in halves or quarters and place in lemon juice until ready to cook. Cook in boiling salted water, uncovered, until tender, 10-15 minutes.

To fry

1. Cut trimmed hearts into thin slices and sauté in butter or olive oil until tender. Season with salt, pepper, and lemon juice.
2. Cut trimmed hearts into thin slices. Dip in seasoned flour and fry in hot oil.

To serve cold

Remove the choke from a cooked, whole artichoke. Season the cavity with salt, pepper, lemon juice, and oil, and fill with seafood or chicken salad, or cooked mixed vegetables in sauce or mayonnaise.

To serve hot

Remove the choke from a cooked, whole artichoke. Season with salt and pepper, and brush with salted butter. Place choke, bottom up, in a casserole with buttered wax paper over the top. Cover and bake at 325°F. for about 20 minutes. The artichokes are then ready to receive any filling you prefer.

ARTICHOKES IN MUSTARD SAUCE/serves 6

12 tiny artichokes
2 cloves garlic
juice of 1 lemon
1/2 cup French dressing (p. 131)
1/4 cup prepared mustard

Pull off the outside leaves of the artichokes, and clip the tips of the rest of the leaves, if you wish. Boil in salted water with the garlic and lemon juice until tender. You may test tenderness by pulling out a leaf. If it pulls out easily, the artichokes are done. Drain upside down. Marinate for several hours in dressing made by blending the French dressing and mustard.

STUFFED ARTICHOKES/serves 6

6 globe artichokes, cooked, cooled
1 small onion, chopped
1 cup chopped ham
5 tablespoons butter
seasoning to taste
2 teaspoons chopped parsley
6 bacon slices

For Sauce
3 cups white wine
1 onion, sliced
1 carrot, sliced
seasoning

Remove chokes from the centre of each artichoke. Sauté onion and ham in the butter, add seasoning and fill the artichokes with the mixture. Wrap a slice of bacon round each artichoke, and secure with a fine string or a small skewer.

Place artichokes close together in a casserole, and add the sauce ingredients. Cover and cook in 350°F. oven one hour. Remove the string or skewer and serve with sauce. Thicken sauce before serving if desired.

Asparagus

Growing asparagus is a long-term project, but the rewards are considerable. As an added benefit, after harvest, the gardener also enjoys the beauty of four to five foot high asparagus fern, which lasts until frost in the fall.

Growing Asparagus

Since starting this vegetable from seed is a two-year project, most gardeners purchase one-year-old asparagus plants from a nurseryman or seedman in the spring and start the bed from these. Remember that asparagus, a member of the lily-of-the-valley family, is one of the perennial vegetables which remain in the garden producing a crop every year.

If starting from seed is more appealing to you, sow the seeds in early spring. First soak the seeds in water with a temperature of 80° to 85° F. for 2 or 3 days to soften the outer hull, then sow them 2 to 3 inches apart in the row. Cover with one inch of soil. Thin out the seedlings so that they are 4 inches apart in the row.

When making the final asparagus bed, space plants as shown in the chart.

In short-season areas, the use of seedling asparagus can be practical. This is carried out by leaving the plants in the row where sown, and then thinning them to 12 inches apart in the row.

Spacing for final bed	Amount	Planting dates
• rows: 4 feet apart • plants: 1-1/2 feet apart • depth: 6 inches	• per person: 30 feet of row	• indoor: March 15 - April 1 (in individual containers) • transplanting dates: May 1 - May 15 • outdoor: May 1 - May 10 • Seedlings emerge in 15 - 21 days • Yield in 4 years • Expected crop 600 spears per 100 feet of row

Cooking Asparagus
1/2 cup or six 6-inch fresh spears = 18 calories

Per serving
6 spears 1/2 to 3/4 inch in diameter
                    or
8 to 10 spears if the asparagus is a separate course.

BASIC PREPARATION

Choose spears that are firm, unwrinkled, and bright green. Scales should lie flat and be tightly closed to a point; the whiter the butt ends, the fresher the asparagus. Fat spears are just as tender as thin ones. Spears should be stored upright, with the butts on dampened absorbent paper or in a half inch of water.

To steam or boil
Divide the asparagus into groups about three inches in diameter. Leave one spear loose, for a cooking test later. Cut all spears the same length. Line up the tips of each group, and tie with a soft white string about 2 inches below the tips, and again about 2 inches from the butt ends.
   Stand each bunch upright in a deep pan. Add enough boiling water to cover stalks to a depth of one inch. Cover and cook about 15 minutes. Remove with tongs, drain, and season.
                    or
Arrange loose stalks in a wide-bottomed pan. Add about a half inch of boiling water. Cover, bring to a boil, and simmer 10 - 12 minutes. Remove as above.

To pan-cook slices—Oriental style
Slice asparagus stalks slantwise in 1/4-inch thick slices; leave tips whole. Melt enough butter or margarine to cover the bottom of a frying pan. Add slices of asparagus. Season if desired. Cover and cook slowly 3 - 5 minutes.

The French cooking method
Peel asparagus, tie it in bundles, and plunge it into a very large kettle of rapidly boiling water. Peeled asparagus cooks more quickly and can be eaten all the way down to the butt. However, the peeling does add to the preparation time.

To serve
As a main luncheon dish: For each portion, top several stalks of asparagus with a fried egg, spoon 1-1/2 tablespoons of melted butter or margarine and some freshly grated Parmesan cheese over all. Top with freshly grated black pepper.
Another luncheon dish: For each portion, top several stalks of buttered asparagus with a thin piece of fried ham, or place the asparagus on top of a slice of ham. Add melted butter and grated cheese.
   Combine 3 tablespoons of prepared mustard, 1 tablespoon of fresh lemon juice, and 6 tablespoons of softened butter. Beat with fork until it is a creamy paste; serve with hot asparagus.

Serve cold asparagus with a good vinaigrette sauce or add a tablespoon of prepared mustard to the vinaigrette sauce (p. 130) and beat it in well. Cold asparagus may also be served with a well-flavoured homemade mayonnaise (p. 134).

Sauces for Hot Asparagus (see also p. 127)
1. Lemon juice and salt, for dieters.
2. Melted butter or lemon butter.
3. Mock hollandaise, or white sauce with lemon flavouring.
4. Plain hollandaise, or hollandaise with whipped cream or beaten egg whites.
5. A mixture of bread crumbs sautéed in butter, chopped parsley and chopped hard-cooked egg.

CHEESE BROILED ASPARAGUS

Sprinkle grated Parmesan or Romano cheese over cooked asparagus and brown under broiler.

ASPARAGUS POLONAISE/serves 6

6 servings of asparagus
1/3 cup fine breadcrumbs
butter
2 hard-cooked eggs, chopped
3 teaspoons chopped parsley

Cook the asparagus. Meanwhile, brown the breadcrumbs in hot butter. Add the chopped eggs and parsley. Spoon over the asparagus before serving.

1965924

ASPARAGUS NORMANDE/serves 6

6 servings of asparagus
1 heaping tablespoon butter
1/2 cup cream
paprika

Cook asparagus. Heat the butter and cream very gently together. Pour over asparagus and dust with paprika.

ASPARAGUS SOUFFLÉ/serves 6

3 tablespoons butter or margarine
3 tablespoons flour
1/2 teaspoon salt
1/8 teaspoon pepper
1 cup milk
6 eggs, separated
1 cup, 1-inch pieces cooked asparagus
1/4 cup finely chopped onion
1 pimiento, chopped

Make a white sauce with the first 5 ingredients (see p. 126) and cool. Beat egg whites until stiff and egg yolks until thick and lemon-coloured. Gradually stir white sauce into egg yolks and fold in egg-whites and remaining ingredients. Pour into a 2 - quart casserole and set in a pan of hot water. Bake in 350°F. oven 45 minutes. Serve at once.

ASPARAGUS SALAD WITH SESAME/serves 6

2 cups cooked asparagus pieces, chilled
1 head lettuce, broken into pieces
2 pimientos, diced
1 green onion, chopped
1/4 cup toasted sesame seeds
1/4 teaspoon pepper

1/4 teaspoon salad seasoning
2 tablespoons lemon juice
1-1/2 tablespoons salad oil

Toss all ingredients together and serve.

Beans

An excellent source of protein, beans are one of our most important vegetables, and can be grown in almost any garden.

Growing Beans

BUSH OR SNAP BEANS

Spacing	Amount	Planting dates
• rows: 2 feet apart • plants: 2 inches apart • depth: 2 inches	• per person: 30 feet of row, 3 ounces of seeds • per 100 feet of row: 10 ounces of seed	• indoor: April 15 - April 30 (in peat pots) • transplanting dates: May 1 - May 15 • outdoor: May 15 - May 31 • Seedlings emerge in 6 - 8 days • Yield in 50 - 70 days • Expected crop 40 quarts per 100 feet of row

This type of bean thrives in warm loam, in areas where nights are dry.

LIMA BEANS

Spacing	Amount	Planting dates
• rows: 2 feet apart	• per person: 30 feet of row, 5 ounces of seed	• indoor: April 15 - April 30 (in peat pots)
• plants: 2 inches apart	• per 100 feet of row: 1 pound of seed	• transplanting dates: May 1 - May 15
• depth: 1-1/2 inches		• outdoor: May 20 - May 31
		• Seedlings emerge in 6 - 8 days
		• Yield in 70 - 80 days
		• Expected crop 25 quarts per 100 feet of row

Only one sowing per season is possible.
When purchasing seeds be certain that they have been chemically treated to ward off possible disease infection.

POLE BEANS

Spacing	Amount	Planting dates
• rows: 3 feet apart	• per person: 30 feet of row, 2 ounces of seed	• indoor: April 15 - April 30 (in peat pots)
• plants: 1 foot apart	• per 100 feet of row: 1/2 pound of seed	• transplanting dates: May 1 - May 15
• depth: 2 inches		• outdoor: May 15 - May 30
		• Seedlings emerge in 6 - 8 days
		• Yield in 60 - 70 days
		• Expected crop: 50 quarts per 100 feet of row

Pole beans grow best when trained on a fence, on poles, or other structures strong enough to withstand the weight.

Cooking Snap Beans

Green beans: 3 -1/3 ounces, raw = *32 calories*
cooked = *25 calories*
Wax beans: 3 -1/3 ounces, raw = *27 calories*
cooked = *22 calories*

BASIC PREPARATION

Wash beans in cold water, sort, and remove stem and top. Leave whole, cut in one-inch pieces, or French cut in thin diagonal pieces.

Cook in one inch of rapidly boiling water for 2 - 3 minutes. Cover and simmer until tender-crisp. Drain, season, add butter or margarine, and serve.

Cooking Lima Beans

3 -1/2 ounces = *123 calories*

BASIC PREPARATION

Cut thin strips from inner edge of pods and remove beans. Cook in one inch of boiling salted water until tender. Drain, add seasoning and butter.

FRUITED BEAN CASSEROLE/serves 6

salt, pepper
1/2 cup melted butter or margarine
1 cup light brown sugar
1 28-ounce can pear halves, drained and cubed
3 cups Lima beans, cooked and drained

Mix together salt, pepper, butter, and sugar. Alternate layers of beans and pears in a 2-quart casserole, spreading each layer with sugar mixture. Cover and bake in 300°F. oven one hour.

FRENCH BEANS LYONNAISE/serves 4

2 onions, chopped
3 tablespoons butter
1 pound green beans, cut French style, cooked until tender
seasoning
parsley, chopped

Sauté onion in butter until golden. Add beans and toss gently. Season and serve hot with chopped parsley.

GREEN BEANS, MAILLANE STYLE/serves 6

2 pounds tiny green beans cooked tender-crisp
3 tablespoons olive or salad oil
1 garlic clove, finely chopped
parsley, chopped

Heat oil and garlic. Add beans and toss until heated. Add parsley and season if necessary.

GREEN BEANS AND MUSHROOMS/serves 6

1/2 pound fresh mushrooms, diced
1 small onion, finely chopped
2 tablespoons butter or margarine
1 pound fresh green beans
3/4 cup water
salt and pepper
1/3 cup heavy cream

Sauté mushrooms and onion in butter. Add beans, water, salt, and pepper. Bring to a boil, cover and simmer slowly until tender. Add cream. Heat — but do not boil.

BEAN SALAD/serves 8

1 pound green beans, or 2 cups frozen beans
1 pound wax beans, or 2 cups frozen beans
1 pound lima beans or 2 cups frozen small lima beans
1 16-ounce can kidney beans
3 green onions, chopped
1 clove garlic, crushed
1/2 cup French dressing (p. 131)
salad greens (optional)

Cut and cook the green and wax beans if using fresh. If frozen, buy cut or French cut beans and cook all the package beans according to directions. Toss all beans together with green onions. Mix garlic with dressing and pour over. Toss again and serve on greens if you wish.

BEAN, ASPARAGUS, AND GRAPE SALAD/serves 4 - 6

1/2 pound green beans, or 1 10-ounce package whole frozen beans
1 pound asparagus, or 2 10-ounce packages frozen asparagus
3/4 to 1 pound grapes
1 head leaf lettuce
juice of 1 lemon
2 tablespoons olive oil
1/2 cup heavy cream
1/2 teaspoon salt
1/8 teaspoon pepper
1/4 teaspoon sugar

Cook beans in salted water until just tender. Rinse them at once in cold water so they will not be overdone.

If using fresh asparagus, tie in 4 - 5 bunches, and cook in one quart of salted water. Remove from water when almost tender. If using frozen, follow package directions, cooking a little less time than recommended.

Refrigerate vegetables.

Pull grapes from stems. Break the greens into bite-size pieces in salad bowl and add asparagus and beans on top. Garnish with grapes. Mix remaining ingredients together thoroughly and pour over as a dressing.

GREEN BEANS WITH ONION AND TOMATO/serves 6

2 pounds fresh green beans cut French style
2 cups canned tomatoes
1/2 garlic clove, mashed
2 tablespoons melted butter or margarine

1 onion, finely chopped
1/2 teaspoon salt
1/8 teaspoon pepper

Combine all ingredients in 1-1/2 -quart casserole and bake, covered, in 325°F. oven 45 minutes

SOUR BEANS

Wash and string wax beans. Cook in boiling salted water until tender. Drain and pack in jars or crocks. Cover with cider vinegar. Add 1/2 cup of sugar for each quart of vinegar used. Season with salt, pepper, and mustard seed, to taste. It is not necessary to seal.

Beets

Children seem to enjoy growing beets, possibly because of the colourful red stems and bulbous root that is often seen bulging out of the soil when ready to harvest.

Growing Beets

Spacing	Amount	Planting dates
• rows: 2 feet apart	• per person: 30 feet of row, 2 packets of seeds	• outdoor: May 1 - July 10
• plants: 2 inches apart		• Seedlings emerge in 7 - 10 days
• depth: 1/2 inch		• Yield in 55 - 70 days
		• Expected crop: 500 roots per 100 feet of row

Many plantings per season are possible.
When thinning seedlings use the culled leaves as table greens. They can be prepared in the same way as spinach.

Cooking Beets
1/2 cup cooked (3 -1/3 ounces) = 34 calories

BASIC PREPARATION

Wash and scrub beets with a brush. Do not break the skin. Remove the leaves except for 1 - 2 inches of stalk.

To boil
Place beets into boiling lightly salted water. Cover and cook until the skins slip off easily.

To bake
Dry scrubbed beets and bake in 350° F. oven until they give a little when pressed with the finger.

HOT BEETS/serves 6

3 cups cooked sliced beets
1 tablespoon butter
    seasoning
2 tablespoons chopped chives
1 teaspoon lemon juice

Toss cooked sliced beets in melted butter. Add seasoning, chopped chives, and lemon juice.

BEETS AU GRATIN/serves 6

1-1/2 pounds beets, parboiled
2-1/2 cups cheese sauce (p. 126)
    1 cup grated cheese
    1 tablespoon butter or margarine

Arrange beets in buttered shallow casserole. Add sauce and grated cheese and dot with butter. Bake in 350° F. oven 15 - 20 minutes.

HARVARD BEETS/serves 6

    2 teaspoons cornstarch
1/3 cup sugar
1/2 teaspoon salt
    dash pepper
2/3 cup vinegar
1/3 cup beet liquid
    3 cups sliced cooked beets
    1 tablespoon butter or margarine

Mix dry ingredients together and add to vinegar and beet liquid. Cook slowly, stirring constantly, until thickened. Add beets and heat thoroughly. Stir in butter just before serving.

BUTTERED BEETS WITH MUSTARD/serves 6

3 tablespoons butter or margarine
1 tablespoon prepared mustard
1 tablespoon tarragon vinegar
3 cups diced cooked beets

Beat first 3 ingredients together. Heat beets and place on serving dish. Add mustard-butter mixture and toss before serving.

BEET AND FRUIT SALAD/serves 6

1/2 pound sliced cooked beets
    1 cup cubed pineapple
    1 apple, peeled, cored and sliced
        sections of 2 oranges
    2 bananas, sliced
1/2 cup Lemon French dressing (p. 131)
    1 cup coarsely chopped peanuts

Mix beets with fruit, working quickly so that the apples and bananas will not darken. Pour Lemon French dressing over and sprinkle peanuts on top.

BEET SALAD/serves 6

    4 to 6 large beets, cooked
    1 onion, sliced thin
1/2 cup mayonnaise
    2 teaspoons tarragon vinegar
1/4 cup heavy cream, whipped

Slice beets, and mix with onion in a salad bowl. Combine mayonnaise with vinegar and fold in whipped cream. Pour sauce over salad and chill.

Broccoli

Broccoli is a member of the cabbage family. The head of the broccoli is the flowering part. It is picked before it is fully grown. The stems and leaves are also eaten.

Growing Broccoli

FOR EARLY SOWING

Spacing	Amount	Planting dates
• rows: 2 feet apart • plants: 2 feet apart • depth: 1/4 inch	• per person: 15 feet of row, 1 pinch of seeds • per 100 feet of row: 3 packets of seeds	• indoor: March 25 - April 10 • transplanting dates: April 15 - May 15 (or after last frost) • outdoor: March 1 - April 10 • Seedlings emerge in 6 - 9 days • Yield in 60 - 70 days • Expected crop: 80 quarts per 100 feet of row

Broccoli should be started as early as conditions permit in order to miss the summer's hottest days at heading time.

FOR LATE SOWING

Spacing	Amount	Planting dates
• rows: 2 feet apart • plants: 2 feet apart • depth: 1/2 inch	• per person: 15 feet of row, 1/2 packet of seeds • per 100 feet of row: 3 packets of seeds	• indoor: May 20 - June 10 • transplanting dates: June 15 - July 10 • outdoor: May 24 - June 24 • Seedlings emerge in 7 - 10 days • Yield in 60 - 70 days • Expected crop: 60 quarts per 100 feet of row

Broccoli can also be sown late to escape the hottest summer heat at heading time.

LATE SEEDING

Late seeding in the field is practical for late summer and fall crops. Sow May 1 to June 1. Plant 2 to 4 seeds per individual separate plant. Sow to a depth of 1/2 to 3/4 inches. Thin to desired spacing in rows when the plants are 2 to 4 inches tall and before crowding occurs.

Cooking Broccoli
1 cup cooked = 44 calories

BASIC PREPARATION

Cut the top portion off each head, usually down to where the branches separate from the central stem. Make all pieces about a half inch thick at the base.

Cut off and discard the tough butt of the central stems, and with a small knife, peel off the outside skin in strips, coming almost up to the flower buds. For quicker cooking, make a half-inch slit through the bottom of each branch.

Wash thoroughly and quickly in cold water. Refrigerate in a covered bowl until ready to cook.

Prepare the sauce and warm the serving dish before cooking the broccoli.

Use in all ways suggested for asparagus. Broccoli heads freeze well.

BUTTERED BROCCOLI/serves 6

3 cups fresh broccoli, cut, or two
   10-ounce packages frozen broccoli
1 cup water
3 tablespoons butter or margarine
3/4 teaspoon onion salt
   prepared mustard

Place broccoli in boiling water, add butter and sprinkle with onion salt. Cook covered until tender-crisp. Serve with prepared mustard.

GOURMET BROCCOLI/serves 6

1 or 2 bunches of broccoli
2 cloves garlic, finely chopped
   salt and pepper
1/2 cup dry white wine
   oil

Cook broccoli until barely tender and drain. Sauté garlic cloves until lightly brown in enough oil to cover the bottom of a large frying pan. Add broccoli and coat with hot oil. Season with salt and pepper to taste. Pour in white wine, and boil down very quickly. Serve the broccoli with pan juices.

BROCCOLI AND HAM CASSEROLE/serves 6

1-1/2 cups fresh broccoli, cut, or one
   10-ounce package frozen cut-up
   broccoli, cooked tender-crisp
1 cup diced cooked ham
6 potatoes, peeled, cooked
2 cups cheese sauce (p. 126)
6 tea biscuits

Combine first 4 ingredients together in a casserole. Cover and bake in 425° F. oven 15 minutes. Uncover, place tea biscuits on top and cook 5 - 8 minutes longer.

Brussels Sprouts

A very hardy plant, Brussels sprouts give particular satisfaction as many pickings from each plant are possible, as is the case with tomatoes. The miniature, cabbage-like vegetables are picked as they mature over several weeks.

Growing Brussels Sprouts

Spacing	Amount	Planting dates
• rows: 2 feet apart • plants: 2 feet apart • depth: 1/4 inch	• per person: 15 feet of row, 1/2 packet of seeds • per 100 feet of row: 3 packets of seeds	• indoor: April 1 - April 25 (in peat pots) • transplanting dates: May 20 - May 30 (or after last frost) • outdoor: May 10 - June 15 • Seedlings emerge in 6 - 9 days • Yield in 70+ days • Expected crop: 60 quarts per 100 feet of row

Two plantings per season are possible. When the sprouts begin to form, remove the growing points of the plants.

When sowing this vegetable, keep a few seeds in reserve to be sown in late August or early September in containers (bushel baskets, or 12-inch-deep wooden boxes) of garden soil which can be removed into a garage or other out-building at the first frost. By this method it is not uncommon to enjoy your own fresh-picked Brussels sprouts with Christmas dinner.

Cooking Brussels Sprouts

1 cup (4 -1/3 ounces) = 60 calories

BASIC PREPARATION

Remove outer leaves. Cut the base of each sprout. Wash well.

To boil
Cook in boiling salted water. Drain and toss with melted butter.

To cook with butter
Partially cook sprouts in boiling salted water. Drain, sauté in butter, and season. Cover and simmer until tender-crisp.

To cook with cream
Partially cook sprouts in boiling salted water. Drain and simmer in butter or margarine until tender-crisp. Cover with fresh cream, bring to a boil and serve.

Curried Brussels sprouts
Partially cook sprouts in boiling salted water. Drain and simmer in butter or margarine until tender-crisp. Toss in a curry sauce and serve surrounded with rice.

Brussels sprouts Milanese
Cook sprouts tender-crisp in boiling salted water and drain. Place in buttered casserole, sprinkle with grated cheese and dribble melted butter. Place under broiler until browned.

Prepare Brussels sprouts with any sauce or garnish used for cauliflower.

SPROUTS AND MUSHROOMS/serves 6

1/4 pound mushrooms, sliced	Sauté mushrooms in butter until tender.
6 tablespoons butter or margarine	Add remaining ingredients and toss.
1 pound Brussels sprouts, cooked tender-crisp, drained	Serve hot.
1/2 teaspoon salt	
1/8 teaspoon pepper	
2 tablespoons cream	

BRUSSELS SPROUTS 'N' POTATO CASSEROLE AU GRATIN/serves 6

1-1/2 quarts Brussels sprouts	Place cooked sprouts in centre of
2 cups mashed potatoes	2-quart casserole. Spoon mashed
1/2 cup grated cheese	potatoes around edge. Top sprouts with
1 cup medium white sauce (p. 126)	remaining ingredients. Brown under broiler.
1 tablespoon butter or margarine, melted	

Cabbage

There are many different varieties of cabbage including red, green, and white cabbage. The cabbage family also includes cauliflower, broccoli, Brussels sprouts, and kohlrabi.

Growing Cabbage

Both early and late-sown cabbage thrive in rich soil as they are heavy feeders.

FOR EARLY SOWING

Spacing	Amount	Planting dates
• rows: 2 feet apart • plants: 2 feet apart • depth: 1/4 inch	• per person: 15 feet of row, 1/2 packet of seeds • per 100 feet of row: 3 packets of seeds	• indoor: March 15 - April 10 • transplanting dates: April 25 - May 10 (or after last frost) • outdoor: May 1 - May 15 • Seedlings emerge in 6 - 9 days • Yield in 70 - 105 days • Expected crop: 50 heads per 100 feet of row

Two plantings per season are possible.

FOR LATE SOWING

Spacing	Amount	Planting dates
• rows: 2 feet apart • plants: 2 feet apart • depth: 1/4 inch	• per season: 15 feet of row, 1/2 packet of seeds • per 100 feet of row: 3 packets of seeds	• outdoor: May 24 - June 10 • Seedlings emerge in 7 - 10 days • Yield in 70+ days • Expected crop: 50 heads per 100 feet of row

Avoid planting late-growing cabbage in areas with a short growing season.

Cooking Cabbage

red, cooked: 3 -1/2" x 4 -1/2" wedge (3 -1/2 ounces) = *27 calories*
white, shredded: 1 cup (3 -1/2 ounces) = *24 calories*
Chinese, raw: 1 cup (3-1/2 ounces) = *16 calories*

BASIC PREPARATION

Various white cabbages are used for sauerkraut. Green cabbage hearts and greens are braised and used in soups. Red cabbage is braised and seldom blanched first.

Cut a cabbage into quarters. Remove the fibrous part of the stem and the coarse outer leaves. Cook in salted water until tender-crisp. Drain thoroughly and slice into serving pieces.

BRAISED CABBAGE/serves 6

2 onions, chopped	*Sauté onion and bacon in butter until*
3 slices bacon, chopped	*brown. Stir in flour. Gradually add stock.*
2 tablespoons butter or margarine	*Bring to a boil and cook until thickened.*
2 tablespoons flour	*Remove hard core from cabbage. If*
2 cups stock or water	*young, add to sauce directly; if not, first*
1 head cabbage cut into 6	*cook for 5 minutes in boiling salted water.*
1 teaspoon thyme	*Place cabbage in sauce, and add season-*
seasoning	*ing. Cover and simmer one hour. Garnish*
parsley	*with chopped parsley.*

HAM, CABBAGE AND TOMATOES/serves 6

1 small cabbage, shredded	*Place cabbage in shallow 2-quart*
6 1-inch-thick serving-size pieces	*casserole and spread ham on top. Mix*
cooked ham	*remaining ingredients and pour over the*
3 cups canned tomatoes	*ham and cabbage. Bake uncovered in*
3/4 teaspoon pepper	*350° F. oven 35 minutes.*
1/2 teaspoon onion salt	
2 teaspoons steak sauce	
2 teaspoons sugar	

"BUBBLE AND SQUEAK"

Combine equal portions of mashed	*well. Heat a little fat in a frying pan and*
potatoes and finely chopped cooked	*brown each side of potato cabbage cake.*
cabbage to form a smooth cake. Season	*Serve hot.*

EASY STUFFED CABBAGE/serves 6

1 cabbage	*Cut off bruised leaves and trim base of*
1 cup stock	*cabbage flat. Scoop out the centre and*
1/2 pound pork sausage meat	*cook in boiling salted water only until*
salt, pepper	*soft. Fill the cavity with sausage meat.*
3 tablespoons breadcrumbs	*Place cabbage in a casserole, pour over*
tomato sauce	*stock and sprinkle with breadcrumbs.*
	Bake, covered, in a 350° F. oven 1-1/2
	hours, removing cover last 15 minutes.
	Serve with heated tomato sauce.

STUFFED CABBAGE LEAVES/serves 6

6 large cabbage leaves
1 small onion, chopped
1/2 pound minced beef
1 egg
1/2 cup quick-cooking oats
1 tablespoon Worcestershire sauce
milk
stock or water
seasoning
tomato sauce

Drop cabbage leaves in boiling water for a few moments to soften them, and then drain. Mix together next 5 ingredients. Moisten with a little milk and season. Place an equal amount of filling on each cabbage leaf and roll up. Arrange the rolls in a greased casserole to prevent sticking, pour over enough stock to cover bottom of casserole. Cover, and bake in 350° F. oven one hour. Drain and serve with heated tomato sauce.

RED AND WHITE CABBAGE SALAD/serves 6

1 small head white cabbage, shredded
1 small head red cabbage, shredded
2 apples, peeled, cored and diced
2 tablespoons vinegar
1 teaspoon sugar
1/2 cup French dressing (p. 131)

Mix the red and white cabbage together. Add the apples, vinegar, and sugar, and toss lightly, then toss in the French dressing.

COLE SLAW/serves 6 - 8

1/2 teaspoon salt
1/2 teaspoon onion powder
1/4 teaspoon pepper
1 tablespoon sugar
1 teaspoon mustard
1 teaspoon celery seed
3 tablespoons wine vinegar
1/3 cup salad oil
4 cups shredded cabbage
1 sweet red or green pepper, chopped
1-1/2 tablespoon minced parsley

Blend all the seasonings with the vinegar and oil in large bowl. Add cabbage and the red or green pepper. Mix thoroughly. Just before serving, sprinkle with minced parsley.

SOUR CREAM COLE SLAW/serves 4

1 small head cabbage
1 cup dairy sour cream
1 tablespoon vinegar
1 tablespoon sugar
1 teaspoon salt
1/2 teaspoon pepper
1/2 teaspoon prepared mustard (optional)

Shred the cabbage fine. Mix the sour cream with vinegar, sugar, salt, pepper. Add mustard if you wish. Fold into the cabbage, mixing thoroughly, and let stand a few hours before serving.

RED CABBAGE

Red cabbage can be cooked in exactly the same way as green cabbage. It also lends itself to pickling.

Carrots

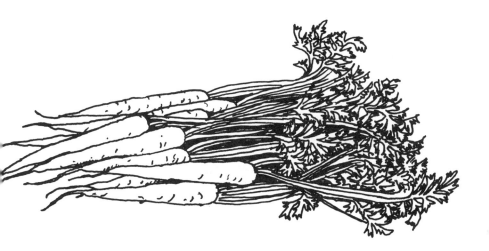

Like other root vegetables, carrots store easily, but are especially delicious eaten raw, straight from the garden.

Growing Carrots

Spacing	Amount	Planting dates
• rows: 2 feet apart	• per person: 30 feet of row, 1 packet of seeds	• outdoor: April 15 - June 1
• plants: 2 inches apart		• Seedlings emerge in 12 - 18 days
• depth: 1/2 inch	• per 100 feet of row: 1/2 ounce of seeds	• Yield in 65 - 75 days
		• Expected crop: 500 roots per 100 feet of row

Many plantings per season are possible.
The proper spacing of the seedlings is extremely important for good growth.

Cooking Carrots

raw, grated: 1 cup (4 ounces) = *45 calories*
cooked: 1 cup (5 ounces) = *44 calories*

BASIC PREPARATION

Remove carrot tops and ends. Scrape or pare and wash. Leave whole, strip, dice, or slice. Cook in one inch of boiling salted water until tender-crisp.

SCANDINAVIAN CARROT SOUFFLÉ/serves 6

1-1/2 pounds carrots, scraped, sliced,
    cooked, mashed
  1 cup stale breadcrumbs
  1 cup milk
  6 tablespoons butter or margarine,
    melted
  3 egg yolks, beaten
1/4 teaspoons salt
  4 egg whites, beaten stiff

Combine carrots, crumbs, milk, and 3 tablespoons butter. Add beaten egg yolks and salt. Fold in whites and turn into 2-quart casserole. Place in a pan of hot water and bake in 350°F. oven 35 - 40 minutes. Serve at once with 3 tablespoons melted butter over all.

CARROTS VICHY/serves 6

1-1/2 pounds young carrots
  3 tablespoons butter or margarine
    salt, pepper
  2 tablespoons cream or milk
    chopped fresh parsley

Toss thinly sliced carrots in hot butter until well coated. Pour into a covered dish, season, and add cream. Cook in 375°F. oven for 30 minutes. Garnish with chopped parsley.

CARROT SCALLOP/serves 6

  4 carrots, peeled, diagonally sliced
  1 onion, peeled, sliced
1/2 teaspoon salt
  2 tablespoons butter or margarine
  1 can condensed cream of mushroom
    soup
  1 soup can water

Place alternate layers of carrots and onions in a shallow 2-quart casserole and top with salt and butter. Blend soup with water and pour over all. Cover and bake in 400°F. oven 35 minutes; uncover and bake an additional 20 minutes.

CARROTS AND MUSHROOMS/serves 6

  4 cups sliced carrots, cooked crisp,
    drained
1/4 pound fresh mushrooms, sautéed
1/2 teaspoon salt
1/8 teaspoon pepper
1/4 cup melted butter or margarine

Mix all ingredients in a 1-1/2-quart casserole. Bake in 350°F. oven for 20 minutes.

CARROT PUDDING/serves 6

  5 eggs, separated
  1 pound carrots, finely chopped
1/2 teaspoon salt
1/2 cup brown sugar
  1 teaspoon lemon juice
1/2 teaspoon grated lemon rind
1-1/2 cups soft bread crumbs
  2 tablespoons melted butter or mar-
    garine

Beat egg whites until stiff. Fold in yolks and remaining ingredients. Grease and crumb top of double boiler and pour in carrot mixture. Cook one hour over simmering water. Unmold and serve with green salad.

Cauliflower

Its very name suggests that it is a flower on a stem. Cook the fleshy parts of the flower and enjoy delightful eating.

Growing Cauliflower

FOR EARLY SOWING

Spacing	Amount	Planting dates
• rows: 2 feet apart • plants: 2 feet apart • depth: 1/4 inch	• per person: 30 feet of row, 1 packet of seeds • per 100 feet of row: 1/2 ounce of seeds	• indoor: March 1 - March 30 • transplanting dates: April 15 - May 15 • Seedlings emerge in 5 - 10 days • Yield in 65 - 70 days • Expected crop: 50 heads per 100 feet of row

FOR LATE SOWING

Spacing	Amount	Planting dates
• rows: 2 feet apart • plants: 2 feet apart • depth: 1/4 inch	• per person: 15 feet of row, 1/2 packet of seeds • per 100 feet of row: 3 packets of seeds	• outdoor: May 24 - June 10 • Seedlings emerge in 7 - 10 days • Yield in 60 - 70 days • Expected crop 100 heads per 100 feet of row

Tie the leaves of the cauliflower over the head when it is nearly mature. The purple types can be left untied.

Cooking Cauliflower
1 cup (3 -1/2 ounces) fresh, raw = 25 calories

BASIC PREPARATION

Cut away the woody base and tough outer leaves. The head may be left whole or broken into flowerets. Wash in cold running water, holding the head or flowerets upside down.

To boil
Place the cauliflower in one inch of boiling water. Add lemon juice or a slice of lemon to keep the cauliflower white. Cook uncovered for five minutes, then cover. Flowerets will take 5 - 10 minutes and heads 15 - 20 minutes. Do not overcook.

To mold
To reform the cauliflower into a head shape after cooking, choose a bowl approximately the same size as the original uncut head. Heat the bowl over hot water, and when the cauliflower is done, pack in flowerets, head down, pouring a spoonful of sauce or butter over as you go. When the bowl is filled, press the cauliflower down with a saucer. Place a heated serving dish upside down over the bowl, and reverse. Remove the bowl. Add sauce or decorate the cauliflower and serve immediately.

SAUTÉED CAULIFLOWER/serves 6

1 medium cauliflower
3 tablespoons butter or margarine
    chopped parsley
    seasoning
	Wash the cauliflower and divide into small flowerets. Heat butter and fry cauliflower carefully until golden brown. Cover and steam-cook on low heat just until tender. Toss in chopped parsley and seasoning.

CAULIFLOWER AND ALMOND BUTTER/serves 6

5 tablespoons butter or margarine 1/2 cup slivered blanched almonds 2 small cauliflower cooked, drained	Sauté almonds in butter until golden and serve over hot cauliflower.

QUICK CHEESEY CAULIFLOWER WITH MUSHROOM SAUCE/serves 6

1 can condensed mushroom soup 1/2 cup grated Cheddar cheese 1 cauliflower, cooked 1 cup browned breadcrumbs chopped parsley	Mix the soup and the cheese together. Heat, stirring constantly, until the cheese has melted and the sauce is very hot. Pour sauce over cauliflower, and sprinkle with breadcrumbs. Brown under the broiler and garnish with chopped parsley.

CAULIFLOWER AND AVOCADO SALAD/serves 6

1 large head cauliflower
1/4 cup vinegar
5 tablespoons salad oil
3/4 teaspoon salt
1/4 teaspoon pepper
3 avocados
1/3 cup coarsely ground almonds
1 small onion, minced
   dash nutmeg
   tomato wedges, radishes, olives
   (garnish)

Cook cauliflower in salted water until tender. Mix half the oil and vinegar with 1/2 teaspoon salt and the pepper, and pour over the cauliflower while it is still warm. Chill. Peel and mash the avocados and mix with remaining oil, vinegar, salt, almonds, and onion. Add nutmeg and any remaining marinade from the cauliflower. Put cold cauliflower on round plate and pour the avocado sauce over. Garnish if you wish with tomato wedges and/or radishes and olives.

MARINATED CAULIFLOWER/serves 6

1 medium cauliflower, separated
   and cooked tender-crisp
1/2 cup olive or salad oil
1/4 cup wine vinegar
1/2 teaspoon salt
1/2 teaspoon pepper
1/4 teaspoon basil
6 anchovy fillets, diced (optional)
2 tablespoons capers
1/4 cup sliced ripe olives
   salad greens

Beat oil together with next four ingredients and pour over cauliflower. Add next three ingredients and toss lightly. Cover and chill 4 - 8 hours, stirring occasionally. Lift cauliflower from marinade and serve on greens with marinade dressing.

CAULIFLOWER SALAD/serves 6

1 large head cauliflower
   salad greens
2 tomatoes
1 green pepper
1/3 cup mayonnaise
1 tablespoon lemon juice
1 tablespoon minced chives and/or
   parsley

Cook cauliflower whole in salted water until it starts to get tender, about 10 - 15 minutes (do not overcook or it will be mushy and fall apart). Drain and chill. Place some salad greens on a deep platter or shallow salad bowl with the cauliflower on top. Peel and slice or cut the tomatoes in eighths and put around the cauliflower. Cut green pepper into strips and put around the salad. Mix mayonnaise with lemon juice; spread thin layer on cauliflower and a little on the tomatoes. Sprinkle chives and/or parsley over all.

Celeriac

Often called knob-celery, celeriac is a dark turnip-rooted type of celery. Only the root is eaten.

Growing Celeriac

Instructions for growing celeriac are almost identical to those for celery. Minor differences in growing methods should be stated on the seed packets.

Cooking Celeriac
3 -1/2 ounces raw = 40 calories

BASIC PREPARATION

Wash celeriac with a vegetable brush. Cut off the top of the root. Peel and cut into slices, julienne, or dice.

To boil
Add to one inch of boiling salted water. Cover and cook 20 - 30 minutes. Drain, season, and serve with butter or cream sauce.

or

Remove top and cook whole without peeling in boiling salted water until tender. Peel, then slice, dice, or julienne.

CELERIAC WITH CHEESE/serves 6

4 roots celeriac salt, pepper 1 cup shredded Cheddar cheese 2 cups thin white sauce (p. 126) 1/2 cup fine dry breadcrumbs, buttered with 3 tablespoons melted butter or margarine.	Cut off celeriac tops, peel roots and dice. Cook in 1-inch boiling salted water about 20 minutes or until tender, drain and place in shallow 2-quart casserole. Mix cheese with hot white sauce until melted, pour over celeriac root and season to taste. Top with buttered crumbs and bake in 375°F. oven until browned.

Celery

Celery is a popular stalk vegetable. The leaves, stalk, and roots are all edible. It is often eaten raw, but can also be boiled, fried, or braised with a sauce.

Growing Celery

Celery does best on specially maintained soils, called mucksoils, which are often drained marshes. Good crops can be produced on fertile, medium-textured mineral soils when water is assured.

Since germination is often poor, heavy seeding is recommended.

FOR EARLY SOWING

Spacing	Amount	Planting dates
• rows: 2 - 3 feet apart	• per person: 15 feet of row, 1/2 packet of seeds	• indoor: March 1 - April 1
• plants: 6 inches apart		• transplanting dates: May 10 - May 20
• depth: 1/8 inch	• per 100 feet of row: 1 packet of seeds	• Seedlings emerge in 15 - 20 days
		• Yield in 120 - 150 days
		• Expected crop 200 plants per 100 feet of row

Only one planting per season is possible.

FOR LATE SOWING

Spacing	Amount	Planting dates
• rows: 2 - 3 feet apart	• per person: 15 feet of row, 1 packet of seeds	• outdoor: May 20 - May 31
• plants: 6 inches apart		• Seedlings emerge in 15 - 22 days
• depth: 1/8 inch	• per 100 feet of row: 2 packets of seeds	• Yield in 120 - 150 days
		• Expected crop: 200 plants per 100 feet of row

Only one planting per season is possible. Late celery should not be sown in areas with a short growing season.

Cooking Celery

1/2 cup (2 ounces) raw = 12 calories

BASIC PREPARATION

The inner stalks are best served raw. Break the stalks apart and wash. Cut into desired lengths, or make celery curls or tiny strips.

To boil
Add diced or sliced celery to one inch of boiling water, stock, or bouillon. Cover and cook for 15 minutes. Season with butter or white sauce (p. 126).

To braise
Place 1-1/2 pounds of 3-inch celery pieces into a mixture of 1/2 cup chicken bouillon, 1/2 teaspoon salt, 2 tablespoons butter or margarine. Cover and simmer 25 minutes.

To fry
Dip pieces of cooked celery into beaten egg, then coat with fine dry bread-crumbs mixed with grated Parmesan cheese. Fry in deep fat 370° F. until browned.

EASY WALDORF SALAD/*serves 4*

2 cups diced apples
1 cup diced celery
1/2 cup mayonnaise
    broken or coarsely chopped
      walnuts
    lettuce

Mix the apple, celery, and mayonnaise and toss. Serve in a chilled bowl. Top with walnuts, and put a border of lettuce around.

APPLE AND CELERY SALAD/*serves 6*

1/2 cup diced apple
1/2 cup diced celery
1/4 cup mayonnaise
1 head lettuce
6 slices bacon

Mix the apple, celery, and mayonnaise. Break the lettuce into bite-size pieces. If using firm lettuce such as iceberg, shred it. Cook the bacon and dice or cut into thin strips. Toss all together, or put half the lettuce in a bowl, add bacon to remaining lettuce, and toss with the apple and celery.

HAM AND CELERY ASPIC/*serves 6*

1 envelope gelatin
1-1/2 pounds cooked ham, ground
1 teaspoon lemon juice
1 cup minced celery
1 onion, grated
1 cup tomato juice
    lettuce

Soften the gelatin in 1/2 cup hot water and pour over the ham. Add remaining ingredients and pour in mold. Chill until set. Unmold on shredded lettuce.

CHICKEN 'N' CELERY SALAD/serves 6

2 cups diced cooked chicken
1 cup chopped celery
1 cup green grapes, cut in halves
2 tablespoons minced parsley
3/4 teaspoon salt
1/4 teaspoon pepper
1-1/2 tablespoons gelatin
1/2 cup hot chicken stock
3/4 cup mayonnaise
2 tablespoons heavy cream

Mix the chicken, celery, grapes and parsley. Season with salt and pepper. Soften gelatin in 1/4 cup cold water. Dissolve in the hot chicken stock and stir into the salad. Combine the mayonnaise with cream, and fold in. Put in a wet mold or in 6 individual molds and chill until set.

BAKED CELERY AND HAM AU GRATIN/serves 6

3 cups celery, cut into julienne strips
3 cups diced cooked ham
2 cups grated Cheddar cheese
1/3 cup melted butter or margarine
1/4 cup flour
1 cup chicken bouillon
1 cup coffee cream
salt, pepper
1/4 cup dry breadcrumbs
1/4 cup melted butter or margarine

Cook celery until tender-crisp, and place in a 2-quart casserole alternately with ham and grated cheese. Stir flour into melted butter, gradually add bouillon and cream. Cook, stirring continuously, until smooth and thickened. Season to taste and pour over the celery and ham mixture. Sprinkle with breadcrumbs and pour melted butter over all. Bake in 350° F. oven 25 minutes.

Chicory (or Succory)

Chicory is a salad green — a member of the endive family. The roots are sometimes roasted and ground for coffee.

Growing Chicory

To grow chicory, follow instructions for the endive.

Cooking Chicory
1/4 small head (1/2 ounce) = 3 calories

BASIC PREPARATION

Trim and wash greens thoroughly. Discard wilted or discoloured leaves. Dry well and chill.
Serve in any way endive is served.

BRAISED CHICORY

2 quarts (2 pounds) chicory, finely chopped	*Sauté chicory in bacon drippings 3 - 5 minutes, stirring constantly. Season to taste.*
2 tablespoons bacon drippings	

Corn

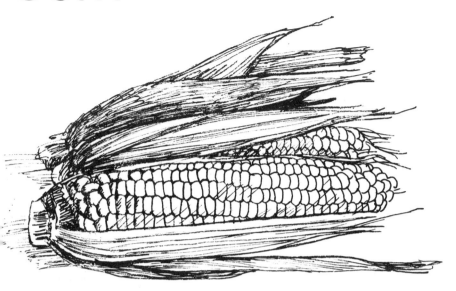

Where space is limited give corn a place on the north side of the garden where its shade won't harm plants that require sunshine. It's fun to grow a few ears of popping corn and make an evening of it when the time comes to do the popping.

Growing Corn

Even in the smallest corn patches, plant two adjacent rows in order that the pollen will be caught on the silks and kernels will form.

EARLY VARIETIES

Spacing	Amount	Planting dates
• rows: 3 feet apart • plants: 8 - 12 feet apart • depth: 1 inch	• per person: 30 feet of row, 2 ounces of seeds • per 100 feet of row, 1/2 pound of seeds	• outdoor: May 10 - May 31 • Seedlings emerge in 5 - 8 days • Yield in 65 - 70 days • Expected crop: 130 ears per 100 feet of row

When thinning the plants, consider the richness of the soil. If the soil is low in plant nutrients, plants should be 12 or more inches apart in the row. Some gardeners have better results planting the seeds on mounds of earth, 6 or 8 seeds to the mound, 24 inches apart in the row.

Two plantings per season are possible.

Spacing	Amount	Planting dates
• rows: 3 feet apart	• per person: 30 feet of row, 2 ounces of seeds	• outdoor: May 10 - May 24
• plants: 1 foot apart	• per 100 feet of row, 1/2 pound of seeds	• Seedlings emerge in 5 - 8 days
• depth: 1 inch		• Yield in 80 - 90 days
		• Expected crop: 100 ears per 100 feet of row

Two plantings per season are not possible in short season districts.

Cooking Corn

2 ears = 1-1/3 cups kernels
1 ear, 5" x 1- 3/4" = 84 calories
1/2 cup fresh kernels = 70 calories
1/2 cup cream style = 80 calories

BASIC PREPARATION

Remove husks and any undeveloped tips. Pull out all silk from between rows of kernels, and rinse cobs in cold water.

Good fresh corn is another vegetable that is at its best when cooked quickly and served simply. The sooner corn is cooked, right after picking, the sweeter it is.

To boil
Put the ears in a pot with cold unsalted water (salt tends to toughen the corn). Bring just to a boil. Then let the ears stand in the boiling water only until tender. Eat at once with salt, pepper, and plenty of sweet butter.

To pan-cook or steam
Soak the ears in cold water 8 - 10 minutes. Place in heavy frying pan with 1/2 cup cold water. Cook covered 5 - 6 minutes. Uncover and cook until water evaporates. Add 1 teaspoon oil for each ear and simmer until tender-crisp.

To roast
Leave husks on but peel back to remove silk. Tie husks securely over cobs. Soak in salted water for 5 minutes and drain. Place over hot fire for 12 - 14 minutes, turning frequently. Or place in 350°F. oven for 20 - 25 minutes. Remove husks and serve.

To roast in aluminum foil
Spread kernels of corn with softened butter or margarine. Wrap tightly in heavy duty foil, and place in 350°F. oven 15 - 18 minutes.

To steam in butter
Just before cooking, cut kernels from 6 ears of corn. Melt 1/2 cup butter in frying pan until just bubbling. Add corn and cook until kernels are heated through. Shake pan well and add salt and pepper to taste. Spoon on hot plates or rounds of toast, fried crisp in butter or oil.

Variations

1. Add 3 tablespoons of finely chopped green pepper and a hint of finely chopped garlic to pan 3 minutes before adding the corn. Blend well.
2. Add 1/2 cup of crisp crumbled bacon.
3. Add 2 tablespoons of finely chopped pimiento and 2 dashes hot Tabasco sauce.
4. Cook the corn in 1/4 cup butter and season to taste. Stir in 4 tablespoons heavy cream and serve immediately.
5. Cook corn in 2 tablespoons butter and stir in 3 tablespoons of Duxelles (see p. 82).

COLOURFUL CORN CASSEROLE/*serves 6*

4 cobs of corn
1 red pepper
1 green pepper
2 onions
    seasoning
6 tomatoes
2 carrots, grated
4 tablespoons butter or margarine
    grated cheese

Cook the corn on the cob until just tender. Strip kernels from cob. Chop red and green pepper, onions, and tomatoes, and sauté with carrots in hot butter. Add corn and stir until corn is reheated. Serve with grated cheese.

BAKED CORN AND TOMATO/*serves 6*

4 cups uncooked corn (from
    the cob)
4 tomatoes, chopped
1/2 onion, chopped
1/2 green pepper, chopped
2 tablespoons butter or margarine
    salt, pepper
1 teaspoon sugar
1 cup breadcrumbs
2 slices bacon, cooked, crumbled

Place one-half of each of first 4 ingredients in a 2-quart casserole. Dot with butter and season with salt, pepper, and sugar. Repeat. Top with breadcrumbs mixed with bacon. Bake in 350°F. oven 45 minutes.

BEEF AND BACON SUCCOTASH/*serves 6*

8 slices bacon, broiled crisp,
    crumbled
1 pound ground beef
2 onions, chopped
3 cups fresh or frozen lima
    beans
1-1/2 cups water
3 cups drained kernel corn
    salt and pepper

Sauté beef and onion in 2 tablespoons bacon dripping, breaking meat up with fork. Add beans and water. Cover and simmer 15 minutes. Add corn and seasonings; simmer 5 minutes longer. Serve with crumbled bacon.

Cucumbers

Cucumbers grow on a vine which can be trained to climb a wire fence or other support, leaving room in the garden for other plants.

Growing Cucumbers

Spacing	Amount	Planting dates
• rows: 5 feet apart • plants: 1 foot apart • depth: 3/4 inch	• per person: 15 feet of row, 1 packet of seeds • per 100 feet of row: 1/2 ounce of seeds	• indoor: April 15 - May 15 (in peat pots) • transplanting dates: June 1 - July 1 • outdoor: May 20 - June 5 • Seedlings emerge in 7 - 10 days • Yield in 70 - 80 days • Expected crop 600 fruits per 100 feet of row

Two plantings per season are possible.

Cucumbers started indoors should be sown in peat-type containers so that the roots will remain undisturbed at transplanting time.

Gardeners sometimes surround each seedling with a cylinder (a 48-ounce can with the top and bottom removed) so that fertilizers can be directed only to the root and main stem. The vine-like foliage of the cucumber can be trained to grow away from other vegetables.

Cooking Cucumbers
one raw cucumber, 7-1/2" x 2" = 25 calories

BASIC PREPARATION

Discard a slice from each end and peel if desired.

To serve raw
Cut into thin slices or strips. Garnish for canapés, or stuff with other fillings.

To marinate
Peel and slice very thin. Chill several hours in a mixture of vinegar, sugar, salt, and pepper.

To boil
Peel and quarter lengthwise or cut into thick slices. Steam or cook in a small amount of boiling salted water until tender (10 - 15 minutes). Drain and season.

To sauté
Cut into 1/4-inch slices. Dip into seasoned flour or egg and breadcrumbs and sauté in butter until golden.

STUFFED CUCUMBERS/serves 6

3 cucumbers	Boil unpeeled cucumbers in a half inch of
1-1/2 cups chopped ham	salted water 5 - 7 minutes. Cut lengthwise
1/2 cup grated Cheddar cheese	and remove seeds. Stuff with a mixture of
1/2 cup breadcrumbs	ham, cheese, and breadcrumbs, mois-
cream	tened with cream. Bake in stock in 350°F.
stock	oven 30 minutes.

CUCUMBERS AU GRATIN/serves 6

2 small cucumbers, sliced	Sauté cucumber in butter until brown.
3 tablespoons butter	Add cheese sauce and heat thoroughly.
1 cup cheese sauce (p. 126)	

CUCUMBER AND SEAFOOD SALAD/serves 4

1/4 pound very fresh white fish, raw	Cut the fish in very thin pieces. Mix the
1/3 cup vinegar	vinegar, ginger, sugar and salt. Pour over
1 teaspoon minced ginger	the fish. Let stand half an hour. Add
2 tablespoons sugar	cucumbers, which have been let stand in
1/2 teaspoon salt	salt, rinsed and drained. Add soy sauce
2 cucumbers, sliced	and mix gently.
1-1/2 tablespoons soy sauce	

STUFFED CUCUMBER SALAD/serves 6

3 cucumbers, cut in half lengthwise	Scrape out the cucumber seeds and mix
6 tablespoons cottage cheese	with the remaining ingredients, except
2 tablespoons minced celery	chives. Taste mixture for seasoning and
2 tablespoons minced green onion	spoon into the cucumber shells. Serve
3/4 teaspoon salt	chilled on the half shell. Or put halves
2 tablespoons mayonnaise	together, chill for several hours, and then
chopped chives	cut into thick slices. Sprinkle with chives
	before serving.

GRATED CUCUMBER SALAD/serves 4

2 cucumbers, grated
2 tablespoons grated onion
1 teaspoon salt
1/4 teaspoon pepper
1 cup yogurt

Drain the grated cucumbers and blend with the other ingredients.

GINGER CUCUMBER SALAD/serves 6

2 large cucumbers, halved
   lengthwise
1/3 cup white vinegar
4 teaspoons sugar
3/4 teaspoon salt
2 slices fresh ginger, slivered

Remove seeds from cucumber and slice thinly. Marinate in remaining ingredients. Chill before serving.

SHREDDED CUCUMBER SALAD/serves 4

2 large cucumbers
2 tablespoons salt
1 tablespoon peanut oil
1 tablespoon soy sauce
1 tablespoon salad oil
1 teaspoon seasoning salt
1 clove garlic, crushed
1/2 teaspoon sugar
1/4 teaspoon pepper

Peel and shred the cucumbers and sprinkle with salt. Let stand in the refrigerator for several hours. Rinse in a sieve under cold running water. Drain thoroughly and squeeze out moisture. Mix all remaining ingredients and pour over the cucumbers.

CUCUMBERS IN SOUR CREAM/serves 6

3 to 4 cucumbers, thinly sliced
3/4 tablespoon salt
1 cup sour cream
1 tablespoon sugar
3 tablespoons vinegar
1/2 teaspoon freshly ground pepper
1 tablespoon minced dill

Sprinkle cucumbers with salt and let stand for at least 2 hours. Rinse in cold water and squeeze out the moisture. Mix rest of ingredients, and fold in the cucumbers and chill.

CUCUMBER ASPIC/serves 4

1 package lemon gelatin
1 envelope unflavoured gelatin
1/4 teaspoon salt
2 cucumbers, peeled
1 tablespoon lemon juice
2 teaspoon chopped onion
3/4 cup mayonnaise

Mix the lemon gelatin and the un-flavoured gelatin with salt and 1 cup boiling water. Stir to dissolve the gelatin. Put the cut-up cucumber in blender with lemon juice and onion, blend until mushy and add to the gelatin. Pour in mold and chill until firm. Serve with mayonnaise.

Eggplant (Aubergine)

Shaped and coloured like giant purple plums, eggplant is attractive as well as delicious.

Growing Eggplant

Spacing	Amount	Planting dates
• rows: 2 feet apart	• per person: 15 feet of row, 1/4 packet of seeds	• indoor: March 15 - April 1
• plants: 2 feet apart		• transplanting dates: June 1 - June 6
• depth: 1/2 inch	• per 100 feet of row: 1 packet of seeds	• Seedlings emerge in 12 - 15 days
		• Yield in 70 - 80 days
		• Expected crop: 400 fruits per 100 feet of row

A warm-season vegetable, eggplants are often restricted to growing in warmer sections. Eggplant should therefore be grown in rich, warm soil situated in a protected area of the garden (where a fence, building, trees, or shrubs will hold back the main force of the prevailing wind). The use of plastic mulches often helps to heat up the soil and make the growing of eggplants more practical in short-season areas.

Cooking Eggplant
2 slices, 1/2 cup (8-1/3 ounces) raw = 60 calories

BASIC PREPARATION

The initial preparation of eggplant will vary with each type of recipe. But to prepare all recipes in which the eggplant is stewed, baked, or fried, the cut or sliced eggplant is salted and left to stand for 30 minutes to remove the excess water. Dry and cook as indicated.

FRIED EGGPLANT

Halve eggplant; scoop out hard centre core and fry the cases until just tender. Fill the cases with a cooked sage and onion dressing. Serve with bacon and sliced carrots.

EGGPLANT AU GRATIN/serves 6

2 onions, coarsely chopped
3/4 cup olive or salad oil
6 tomatoes, peeled, seeded and chopped
2 eggplants, sliced
salt, pepper
3/4 teaspoon dried thyme
1 tablespoon flour
grated Swiss cheese

Sauté onion in oil. Add tomatoes and cook 5 - 8 minutes. Add eggplants and seasonings. Simmer, covered for 15 minutes. Uncover and continue simmering until eggplant is tender but not mushy. Sprinkle with flour and blend into the juices. Add the grated cheese, and place under broiler for a few moments to melt the cheese.

CLASSIC RATATOUILLE/serves 6

1/3 cup salad oil
2 large onions, sliced
3 cloves garlic, chopped
2 small eggplants, cubed
4 small zucchini, sliced
2 green peppers, cut into strips
1 head of fennel, sliced (optional)
2-1/2 cups chopped tomatoes
1 teaspoon dried basil
1 teaspoon salt
1/4 teaspoon pepper
1/2 teaspoon chopped parsley

Sauté onions and garlic in oil. Add eggplant, zucchini, peppers and fennel. Mix well over a brisk heat. Add tomatoes, seasonings, and parsley. Cover and simmer for approximately one hour, stirring occasionally. Remove cover. Cook down until most of the liquid has evaporated and the mixture is thick. Serve hot or serve cold with additional oil and a little vinegar.

VARIATIONS

1. Add 2 celery hearts cut into thin slices.
2. Thirty minutes before the ratatouille is done, add 1 pound small whole mushrooms or 1 pound of large mushrooms, sliced.
3. Substitute 1 or 2 sliced cucumbers for the zucchini.

STUFFED EGGPLANT/serves 6

3 medium eggplants
1/2 teaspoon salt
3 teaspoons salad oil
1/2 cup diced cooked bacon
2 tablespoons chopped parsley
2 tomatoes, skinned, chopped
1/2 cup fresh breadcrumbs
seasoning
1 cup grated Cheddar cheese
2 tablespoons cooked onion, finely chopped

Wash eggplant, remove stalk, and cut in half lengthwise. Cut around each half eggplant 1/4 inch from the skin and then score the surface lightly to ensure even cooking. Sprinkle with salt and oil. Put on a greased baking pan in 400°F. oven 15 - 20 minutes. Make stuffing by mixing all the ingredients together. Scoop out half flesh from centre of cooked eggplant, chop up and add to stuffing. Fill eggplant cases with stuffing, sprinkle with grated cheese and return to oven for 15 minutes. Serve hot with cheese sauce (p.126).

Endive and Escarole

Endive is delicious in salads, either alone or combined with watercress or other greens. It is also tasty as a cooked vegetable.

Escarole is a type of endive with broad waxed leaves and is often used interchangeably with endive.

Growing Endive and Escarole

Endive and escarole should be sown either as early as possible in the spring, or sown late to be grown as a fall crop.

FOR EARLY SOWING

Spacing	Amount	Planting dates
• rows: 2 feet apart • plants: 9 inches apart • depth: 1/2 inch	• per person: 15 feet of row, 1/2 packet of seeds • per 100 feet of row: 2 packets of seeds	• indoor: March 1 - April 1 • transplanting dates: April 15 - May 1 • outdoor: May 1 - May 10 • Seedlings emerge in 10 - 14 days • Yield in 90+ days • Expected crop: 130 plants per 100 feet of row

Two plantings per season are possible.

FOR LATE SOWING

Spacing	Amount	Planting dates
• rows: 2 feet apart • plants: 9 inches apart • depth: 1/4 inch	• per person: 15 feet of row, 1/2 packet of seeds • per 100 feet of row: 2 packets of seeds	• outdoor: June 1 - June 20 • Seedlings emerge in 10 - 14 days • Yield in 90+ days • Expected crop: 130 plants per 100 feet of row

Two plantings per season are possible.

Cooking Endive

45 leaves (4 ounces) raw = 22 calories

BASIC PREPARATION

Endive can be stored in the refrigerator for up to 7 days if it is first wrapped in slightly dampened paper towels and placed in a plastic bag.

To prepare, shave any discoloured bits from root end of each endive with a small knife. Do not loosen the outer leaves. A slightly bitter taste is concentrated in the root; core a cone-shaped piece out of the root. Run cold water over the endives, and drain.

Again, because of the slighlty bitter taste, blanch endives 10 minutes in boiling salted water before proceeding to any recipe.

BRAISED ENDIVE/serves 6

6 endives, blanched
1/3 cup butter or margarine
1/2 cup thickened, seasoned chicken
    stock
1/2 teaspoon pepper

Sauté endives in butter and add rest of ingredients. Cover and heat slowly for 20 minutes, turning once.

BRAISED ENDIVES SIMMERED IN CREAM/serves 6

6 endives, blanched
1/3 cup butter or margarine
3/4 cup heavy cream
    salt and pepper
    lemon juice
1 tablespoon butter or margarine
    chopped parsley

Cover sautéed endives with 1/2 cup heavy cream. Simmer uncovered 10 minutes, basting. Place in warm serving dish, add 3 tablespoons cream to pan, thicken, and season with salt, pepper and a few drops of lemon juice, stirring constantly. Stir in softened butter or margarine, pour over endive and garnish with parsley.

ORIENTAL ENDIVE/serves 6

2 cups water
2 eggs
2 cups flour
6 endives, blanched

Blend together first three ingredients into a lumpy batter. Dip dry endive leaves into batter and fry in hot deep fat (360°F.) for 2-3 minutes. Serve with a soy sauce dip.

ENDIVE SALAD I/serves 4

1 pound endive
10 anchovies
1/2 cup chopped watercress
1/4 cup French dressing (p. 131)

Wash endive and trim the root ends. Pull off a few outside leaves and put them in a salad bowl. Cut centre in quarters lengthwise, and place pieces on top of leaves. Cut up 6 of the anchovies and mix them with watercress and French dressing. Pour over salad and garnish with remaining anchovies, rolled.

ENDIVE SALAD II/serves 4

1 pound endive	Wash endive and remove wilted leaves.
few leaves soft lettuce	Cut each head into quarters lengthwise.
1/4 cup French dressing (p. 131)	Place on greens. Serve with dressing
1 hard-cooked egg, grated	poured over and garnished with egg.

Cooking Escarole
30 leaves (3 -1/2 ounces) raw = 20 calories

BASIC PREPARATION

Soak the escarole to remove sand. Separate leaves and remove tiny roots.

BRAISED ESCAROLE/serves 6

3 medium heads escarole, finely chopped	Sauté escarole in butter. Cover for 5 minutes. Season and serve.
2 tablespoons butter	
salt, pepper	

MIXED GREEN SALAD/serves 8

1 head escarole	Wash and dry greens thoroughly. Break
1 head romaine	escarole and romaine into bite-size
4 to 5 heads endive	pieces and cut up the endive. Put greens
2 tablespoons minced chives	in bowl and sprinkle with chives and pars-
1/2 cup minced parsley	ley. When ready to serve, pour dressing
1/2 cup French dressing (p. 131)	over and toss thoroughly. Don't use too
1/4 cup grated Cheddar cheese or Parmesan cheese	much dressing, just enough to coat greens. Sprinkle with cheese.

HEARTY ESCAROLE AND LENTIL SOUP/serves 6

3 tablespoons olive or salad oil	Sauté onion, garlic, and parsley in oil.
1 onion, chopped	Add escarole, cover and simmer 15 min-
1 clove garlic, chopped	utes. Add to lentils, season and sprinkle
1 tablespoon chopped parsley	with cheese. Mixture should be moist
1 pound escarole, washed, drained, cut into 1-inch pieces	and soupy.
1 pound lentils, soaked, cooked until tender and liquid nearly absorbed	
salt	
1/4 cup grated Romano cheese	

Fennel

Fennel is a double-header vegetable. Its seeds are used as medicine; its leaves as a flavouring in sauces, etc.

Growing Fennel

Fennel is an aromatic plant of the carrot family and is grown in the same manner as carrots. Minor changes in growing methods are indicated on the seed container.

Cooking Fennel
1/2 pound = 58 calories

BASIC PREPARATION

Cut off the feathery top and trim off the outer stalk. Cut off the hard base and slice with the grain. Cover with boiling salted water or braise in bouillon until tender. Serve with butter.

BAKED FENNEL/serves 6

3 heads fennel, trimmed, quartered,
   cooked tender-crisp, drained
4 tablespoons melted butter
   or margarine
3 tablespoons fine dry breadcrumbs
2 tablespoons grated Parmesan cheese
1 hard-cooked egg, chopped
1 tablespoon chopped fennel
   leaves
   paprika

Arrange cooked fennel in shallow greased casserole. Top with 2 tablespoons melted butter. Combine remaining butter with the next four ingredients and add to fennel. Sprinkle with paprika and bake in 450°F. oven 10 minutes.

Fiddleheads

Fiddleheads are edible ferns that grow on the shores of northern lakes and streams. They are similar in flavour to a combination of asparagus and broccoli.

Growing Fiddleheads

This popular fern can only be grown in certain areas and cannot be considered as a general garden vegetable.

Cooking Fiddleheads

BASIC PREPARATION

Remove brown sheath and scales. If stem is crisp, leave it attached to the head. Wash in lukewarm water several times. Soak in salted cold water 30 minutes and drain.

Tender ferns can be served raw in salads, and dressed with vinegar and lemon juice.

To cook
Cook in boiling salted water 10 - 15 minutes (1 cup of water for 2 pounds fiddleheads). Drain.

or

Steam 3 - 5 minutes, and serve with salt, pepper, butter, hollandaise, or other sauce.

Kale

Kale is a vitamin-rich member of the cabbage family. It ranges in colour from green to reddish or purplish shades and varies in size.

Growing Kale

Spacing	Amount	Planting dates
• rows: 2 feet apart • plants: 2 feet apart • depth: 1/4 inch	• per person: 5 feet of row, 1/2 packet of seeds	• indoor: April 1 - April 15 • outdoor: May 1 - May 10 (short growing season) June 15 - July 1 (average or long growing season) • Seedlings emerge in 6 - 9 days • Yield in 55 - 60 days • Expected crop: 50 plants per 100 feet of row

Only one planting per season is possible.
The quality of kale improves after the first light touch of frost in the fall.

Cooking Kale
3 ounces (2/3 cup) raw = 38 calories

BASIC PREPARATION

Rinse well in cold running water. Kale can be used in any way spinach is prepared, but the leaves should be chopped.

COUNTRY STYLE KALE/serves 6

3 pounds kale, cooked, drained,
    chopped
5 tablespoons bacon drippings
2 tablespoons sweet pickle relish
    salt, pepper

Stir kale in hot bacon dripping. Add relish. Heat thoroughly and season.

KALE WITH BACON AND OATMEAL/serves 6

1/4 pound bacon, diced, cooked
2-1/2 cups water
    3 pounds raw kale, chopped
    1 cup cooked oatmeal

Add water and chopped kale to bacon.
Simmer 15 minutes. Stir in oatmeal and
season with salt and pepper.

Western Style
Leave out oatmeal, add
    1 cup grated onion
    3/4 teaspoon basil
1-1/4 teaspoon salt
1-1/4 teaspoon pepper

and cook as above. Garnish with lemon.

KALE SOUFFLÉ

1 pound cooked kale, finely
    chopped
2 tablespoons butter
2 tablespoons flour
1/3 cup milk
    seasonings
4 eggs, separated
1/2 cup grated Parmesan cheese
    (can be omitted)

Heat butter. Stir in flour and cook several
minutes. Add milk, kale, and seasonings.
Beat in egg yolks and cheese. Fold in
stiffly beaten egg whites. Pour into
soufflé dish and bake in 375°F. oven 30 -
35 minutes.

KALE, POTATOES AND SAUSAGE/serves 6

4 pounds potatoes, peeled and
    quartered
4 pounds kale, stripped, cooked,
    drained, minced
5 tablespoons shortening
3/4 teaspoon salt
1 pound knockwurst sausage,
    heated

Half cover potatoes with water. Add kale,
shortening, and salt. Cover and simmer
20 minutes, until quite dry. Top with
knockwurst.

Kohlrabi

Kohlrabi can be cooked and eaten in almost the same way as turnip. It resembles a small-sized turnip with celery-like stems and leaves arising from several points on the root (the root being the edible part).

Growing Kohlrabi

Spacing	Amount	Planting dates
• rows: 2 feet apart	• per person: 5 feet of row, 1/2 packet of seeds	• outdoor: May 1 - July 1
• plants: 4 inches apart		• Seedlings emerge in 10 - 12 days
• depth: 1 inch	• per 100 feet of row: 1/2 packet of seeds	• Yield in 60+ days
		• Expected crop: 300 heads per 100 feet of row

Three plantings per season are possible.
The best time to harvest kohlrabi is when the heads are slightly smaller than tennis balls.

Cooking Kohlrabi

All recipes given for turnip and for celeriac can be used for this vegetable.

KOHLRABI À LA PAYSANNE/serves 6

1 kohlrabi
2 tablespoons shortening
1/3 cup onion, chopped
1-1/2 cups cooked pork, cubed
 salt, pepper
1/2 cup stock
1/2 cup white wine (optional)

Cut kohlrabi into slices, peel. Sauté in shortening with chopped onion. Add cubes of cooked pork, and season to taste with salt and pepper. Moisten with stock and white wine and simmer until hot.

Leeks

In many places it is traditional to "go a-leeking" or join a "leek festival" in early spring when the forests are abundant with these fresh, onion-like plants. To "go a-leeking" is to enter the forest armed only with a shaker filled with salt and an old-fashioned desire to devour all the leeks one can hold. The effect is said to be similar to granny's spring tonics.

Growing Leeks

The leek does not form a bulb but is used like green onions for its stem and leaves. It grows well under conditions unfavourable to the onion.

Spacing	Amount	Planting dates
• rows: 2 feet apart • plants: 6 inches apart • depth: 1/2 inch	• per person: 5 feet of row, 1/2 packet of seeds • per 100 feet of row: 1/2 ounce of seeds	• indoor: March 10 - March 25 • transplanting dates: April 15 - May 10 • Seedlings emerge in 7 - 10 days • Yield in 150 days • Expected crop: 200 stems per 100 feet of row

Only one planting per season is possible.
To create a more appetizing table food, the stems can be bleached by banking them with earth.

Cooking Leeks
1 average leek = 17 calories

Leeks are mainly used as a condiment, but can be prepared in various ways as a vegetable.

BASIC PREPARATION

Wash, trim off the greater part of the green ends, leaving the white lower part. Take off the outside skin and wash.

To boil
Tie in bunches like asparagus and cook in boiling salted water. Drain, dry and serve like asparagus.

To deep-fry
Cut leeks into uniform chunks and parboil in salted water for 8 - 10 minutes. Marinate for 30 minutes in oil, lemon juice, salt, and pepper. Then dip in thin batter and deep-fry in 375°F. fat until crisp and golden.

BRAISED LEEKS

Clean the leeks well and poach. Reheat in butter and serve.

Variations
1. Poach leeks until just tender. Remove from the broth, and wrap with strips of partially cooked bacon. Place on a rack and bake in 350°F. oven until the bacon is crisp.
2. Chill the cooked leeks in the broth. Drain and arrange in a serving dish.

Add a good vinaigrette sauce or French dressing, and top with strips of anchovy.
3. Au gratin: Parboil white part in boiling salted water and drain. Cook covered in butter or margarine until tender-crisp. Place in buttered casserole and sprinkle with grated cheese and melted butter, and brown under broiler.

LEEK SOUP AU GRATIN/serves 6

6 leeks, sliced
1/3 cup uncooked rice
4 cups chicken bouillon
salt, pepper
1/3 pound grated Swiss cheese
1-1/4 tablespoons white wine

Place leeks and rice in a saucepan. Cover with water and simmer until rice is tender. Add bouillon, bring to a boil and season to taste. Melt cheese in wine in top of double boiler, mixing well. Place a generous spoonful of cheese mixture in each serving of soup.

LEEK, BEAN AND BACON SAVOURY/serves 6

6 slices bacon, halved
4 medium-sized leeks
3 tablespoons butter
1 19-ounce can baked beans
2 hard-cooked eggs, sliced

Roll up bacon pieces and thread on thin skewers. Fry until lightly crisp. Remove and keep hot. Cut well-washed and drained leeks into 1/2-inch slices. Add butter to bacon fat in pan. Add leeks and sauté until tender-crisp. Remove. Stir baked beans into fat in pan. To serve, heap beans into middle of serving dish, top with the bacon rolls, surround with leeks and garnish with slices or wedges of egg.

Lettuce

Lettuce is the easiest salad-maker in the garden. Pick as much as you require for instant use.

Growing Head Lettuce

Head lettuce should be sown either early or late whenever growth is best in your locality; heading does not occur during the hottest part of the summer.

FOR EARLY SOWING

Spacing	Amount	Planting dates
• rows: 2 feet apart	• per person: 15 feet of row, 1/4 packet of seeds	• indoor: March 10 - March 25
• plants: 1 foot apart		• transplanting dates: April 15 - May 10
• depth: 1/4 inch	• per 100 feet of row: 2 packets of seeds	• outdoor: April 10 - May 24
		• Seedlings emerge in 6 - 8 days
		• Yield in 75 - 85 days
		• Expected crop: 100 heads per 100 feet of row

Many plantings per season are possible.

FOR LATE SOWING

Spacing	Amount	Planting dates
• rows: 2 feet apart	• per person: 15 feet of row, 1/4 packet of seeds	• outdoor: July 20 - August 1 (mild climates)
• plants: 1 foot apart		July 1 - July 15 (short growing season)
• depth: 1/4 inch	• per 100 feet of row: 2 packets of seeds	• Seedlings emerge in 6 - 8 days
		• Yield in 80 - 90 days
		• Expected crop: 100 heads per 100 feet of row

One planting per season is possible.
The best times for indoor sowing are the same as for the early-sown head lettuce.

Growing Leaf Lettuce

Spacing	Amount	Planting dates
• rows: 2 feet apart	• per person: 15 feet of row, 1/4 packet of seeds	• outdoor: April 10 - August 1
• plants: 1 foot apart		• Seedlings emerge in 6 - 8 days
• depth: 1/4 inch		• Yield in 40 - 45 days
		• Expected crop: 100 heads per 100 feet of row

Many plantings per season are possible.

Leaf lettuce is generally much more tender if it is not thinned, but rather left to grow closely rooted together and crowded in the row.

Cooking Lettuce
2 large or 4 small leaves = 7 calories

BASIC PREPARATION

Wash thoroughly and separate leaves. When using pieces, tear lettuce rather than cutting it. All common varieties of lettuce can be eaten raw in salads.

COOKED LETTUCE/serves 6

1 head of lettuce water spring onions shallots chives, chopped	*Wash the lettuce and divide into 6 portions. Put into boiling salted water together with a few spring onions, shallots, chopped chives and cook until just tender. Strain and toss with melted butter.*

EASY BRAISED LETTUCE/serves 6

1 large lettuce or 2 medium ones 1 sliced onion 1 tablespoon fat 2 tablespoons flour 1-3/4 cups brown stock or gravy 2 tablespoons chopped bacon, fried seasoning	*Wash and dry lettuce and divide into serving pieces. Sauté onion in fat, add flour and cook for several minutes. Add stock, bring to boil and cook until thickened. Add chopped bacon, seasoning and lettuce, and simmer gently in a covered pan for about 35 minutes.*

ROMAINE SALAD BOWL/serves 6

2 heads romaine 2 bunches leaf lettuce 2 large tomatoes, peeled, cut in wedges 1 cucumber, sliced 1 avocado, peeled, sliced (optional) 6 green onions, chopped 1/3 cup French dressing (p. 131) 1/2 teaspoon dry tarragon or chervil	*Tear the romaine and lettuce into bite-size pieces into a salad bowl. Add the tomatoes, cucumber, avocado, and onions, and toss with French dressing, and tarragon or chervil.*

WILTED LETTUCE / serves 6

bacon dripping
8 green onions, sliced
1 tablespoon sugar
1/3 cup vinegar
1/2 teaspoon pepper
2 heads lettuce, washed, leaves
  separated
6 slices bacon, chopped and fried

Sauté onions in bacon dripping. Add next 3 ingredients, cook for 3 minutes and pour over lettuce. Mix lightly and sprinkle with bacon.

WILTED LETTUCE SALAD / serves 4

4 slices bacon cooked crisp,
  crumbled
1/3 cup sugar
1/2 teaspoon salt
1/2 cup vinegar
soft lettuce
2 hard-cooked eggs

Add sugar, salt and vinegar to bacon drippings and add 1/4 cup water. When this comes to boil, pour over greens, which have been broken into pieces, and toss. Sprinkle coarsely chopped eggs and crumbled bacon over top.

CAESAR SALAD / serves 6

1 clove garlic, crushed
3/4 cup olive or salad oil
8 cups mixed salad greens; head
  lettuce, watercress, leaf lettuce,
  endive, etc.
1 teaspoon Worcestershire sauce
1 teaspoon salt
1/4 teaspoon freshly ground pepper
1 egg, coddled
1/4 cup lemon juice
3 ounces Roquefort or Bleu
  cheese, crumbled
2 cups croûtons, toasted or fried

Add garlic to the oil and let stand several hours. Tear salad greens into bite-size pieces. Put into large bowl with oil and seasoning. Open the egg (cooked for 1 minute only) onto the greens. Sprinkle with lemon juice and toss until all greens are coated with oil and seasoning. Add cheese and toss again. Top with croûtons.

TOSSED GREEN SALAD WITH RADISHES / serves 6

1 head lettuce
8 radishes, sliced
4 tomatoes, peeled, sliced
2 hard-cooked eggs
3 tablespoons chopped chives
1/4 cup French dressing (p. 131)

Wash and dry the lettuce and break into bite-size pieces. Put lettuce in salad bowl and add radishes and tomatoes. Chop the eggs, keeping yolks and whites separate. Top vegetables with chopped egg, putting the yolk in centre and white around edge. Sprinkle with chives. Pour dressing over and toss at the table.

TOSSED GREEN SALAD / serves 4

4 cups assorted salad greens
2 teaspoons minced parsley
1/3 cup French dressing (p. 131)
3 tablespoons grated Parmesan
  cheese

Break greens into pieces and place in a large bowl. Mix parsley into dressing. Pour over the greens and toss. Top with cheese.

Vegetable Marrow

Few are the vegetables that can take the place of the main dish as well as can vegetable marrow. Each marrow provides many servings.

Growing Vegetable Marrow

This vegetable is grown in exactly the same manner as squash. Any minor changes in growing procedure will be listed on the seed packet.

Cooking Vegetable Marrow
3-1/2 ounces, raw = 18 calories

BASIC PREPARATION

After washing, the marrow may be peeled or left in its skin. Remove seeds and halve, dice, or slice, or leave whole. Boil, pan fry, mash or stuff.

To roast
Peel the marrow and cut into large pieces. Remove seeds. Put pieces into hot fat in roaster and bake in a 350°F. oven 40 minutes.

To fry
Peel and cut the marrow into rings. Remove seeds. Fry in shallow fat until tender and brown.

STUFFED MARROW

Partially cook unpeeled, whole marrows. Halve, remove seeds, and stuff with one of the following:

1. *Fried onion, tomatoes and cooked rice.*
2. *Left-over cooked meat, minced and blended with a thick sauce, fried onion, tomatoes and capers.*
3. *A vegetarian stuffing of a thick cheese sauce with diced cooked vegetables.*
4. *Grilled bacon diced with sausage meat.*

Heat thoroughly in 350°F. oven.

Mushrooms

Growing mushrooms is in truth not a gardening project, but rather a hobby, or a labour of love. Mushrooms cannot be grown under normal garden conditions, but must be provided with special structures. It is becoming quite popular to keep miniature mushroom farms in cellars or basements of homes.

Mushrooms are not vegetables, but are growths of fungus. As such, they do not have root systems, nor can they convert sun's energy into food. They must instead attach themselves to other growing organisms and parasitically steal energy. The odour of fermenting (or rotting) mushroom beds is sometimes a factor in deciding against raising mushrooms indoors.

Cooking Mushrooms
1/2 cup (1-2/3 ounces) = 8 calories

BASIC PREPARATION

Fresh mushrooms should be white with firm caps and beige stems.

Wipe the mushrooms with damp cloth; rinse and dry quickly. It is not necessary to peel them. Cut into slices crosswise or lengthwise, or use caps whole and slice or chop the stems. To prevent mushrooms from darkening during cooking, sprinkle with a little lemon juice.

To sauté
Add whole or sliced mushrooms to very hot butter and cook only until lightly browned on each side.

To sauté canned mushrooms, drain first and reserve liquid for sauces, soups, casseroles, etc. Sauté mushrooms before adding to almost any food; this gives a more distinctive flavour.

Note: When substituting canned mushrooms for fresh mushrooms,
1 pound fresh = 6-ounce can.

To sauté caps for canapés
Sauté mushrooms quickly in butter, round side down, about 3 minutes; turn and sauté 4 minutes.

CREAMED MUSHROOMS/serves 6

2 cups mushrooms, sliced
2 tablespoons flour
1-1/2 cups milk
2 tablespoons butter or margarine
2 tablespoons cream
salt
pepper
lemon

Simmer mushrooms in milk until just tender. Blend a little flour with cold milk. Add to the mushrooms and cook until thickened. Put in butter and cream, season and add a squeeze of lemon. Serve with toast or bread and butter.

EASY MARINATED MUSHROOMS/serves 4 - 6

1 pound small mushrooms
2 tablespoons olive oil
1/2 cup French dressing (p. 131)
1 garlic clove, halved

Sauté mushrooms in oil, and cover with dressing. Add garlic. Refrigerate overnight and serve on toothpicks.

DUXELLES

This is a delicious addition to many vegetable dishes as well as fine seasoning for sauces and eggs. It will keep in the refrigerator for 14 days, and is also good when frozen.

1/2 cup butter or margarine
2 pounds mushrooms, chopped very fine (stems and all)
1 clove garlic, finely chopped
1 small onion, finely chopped
salt

Sauté mushrooms, garlic and onion in butter. Cook very slowly, stirring occasionally, until liquid is cooked out and the mushrooms are fairly black in colour. Add more butter if needed and season with salt to taste. Store in a jar or crock.

MUSHROOM 'N' CELERY SALAD/serves 6

3/4 pound mushrooms
1 head celery
1/2 cup olive oil
1 teaspoon salt
1/4 teaspoon pepper
lettuce leaves

Wipe mushrooms and remove stems (use stems for soup or sauce, do not throw away). If mushrooms are not pure white, peel the caps. Slice thinly across the head making half oval slices. Wash the celery, pull the stalk apart and cut across making slices the width of the mushrooms. They will be similar in shape. Mix mushroom and celery pieces together. Blend the oil, lemon juice, salt and pepper and toss gently into salad. Chill and serve on lettuce.

MARINATED MUSHROOM SALAD/serves 6

1/2 pound fresh mushrooms, sliced lengthwise through stem
1 medium onion, thinly sliced
1/3 cup salad or olive oil
1/4 cup tarragon vinegar
1/8 teaspoon Tabasco sauce
1/2 teaspoon salt

2 teaspoons minced parsley
1 head lettuce, separated, washed
1 large tomato, cut into wedges

Mix first 7 ingredients. Cover and let stand 4 hours. Put lettuce and tomato pieces in a large bowl and add marinated vegetables. Toss lightly.

Okra

Okra is closely related to cotton and does best in areas where the summers are long and hot. A boon to soup-makers, okra is famous as the chief ingredient in gumbo.

Growing Okra

Spacing	Amount	Planting dates
• rows: 2 feet apart	• per person: 15 feet of row, 1 packet of seeds	• indoor: April 15 - April 20
• plants: 1 foot apart	• per 100 feet of row: 1 ounce of seeds	• transplanting date: June 1
• depth: 1 inch		• outdoor: May 20 - May 31
		• Seedlings emerge in 8 - 12 days
		• Yield in 50 - 60 days
		• Expected crop: 600 pods per 100 feet of row

Two plantings per season are possible.

Cooking Okra

3-1/2 ounces, boiled and drained = 24 calories
1/4 cup frozen = 36 calories

BASIC PREPARATION

Scrub pods and cut off stems. If desired, slice.

To boil
Cook covered in 1/2 to 1 inch of boiling salted water 10 - 15 minutes, or steam until tender. Serve with melted butter, hollandaise, or butter sauce.

To fry
Dip slices into a mixture of egg and water. Then coat with breadcrumbs. Fry 3 - 4 minutes.

BAKED OKRA/serves 6

2 cups cooked okra 1 egg, beaten 1/2 teaspoon salt 1/2 cup cream 1/2 cup milk 1 cup whole kernel corn 1 cup buttered breadcrumbs	Mix first 6 ingredients together, and pour into a buttered casserole. Top with crumbs. Set in pan of water and bake in 350°F. oven 40 - 45 minutes.

OKRA AND TOMATOES WITH LEMON/serves 6

1-1/2 pounds small fresh okra 1/2 cup olive or salad oil 4 onions, peeled and coarsely chopped 2 garlic cloves, peeled and chopped 4-1/2 cups (approx.) stewed tomatoes salt, pepper 2 teaspoons coriander, tied in cheesecloth bag lemon wedges	Trim cone-shaped tops from okra. Wash and dry thoroughly. Sauté the onions and garlic in oil. Cook gently until tender. Add okra. Cook, tossing lightly until slightly browned. Add next 4 ingredients. Cover, and simmer gently until okra is tender. Remove the bag. Serve with lemon wedges, hot or cold.

FRIED OKRA/serves 6

1-1/2 pounds fresh okra, sliced 1/4-inch thick 1/2 teaspoon salt 1/4 teaspoon pepper 1/2 cup cornmeal 1 tablespoon flour 3 tablespoons shortening or bacon dripping	Sprinkle okra with salt and pepper; coat with cornmeal and flour. Sauté in hot fat until golden.

Onions

The onion is a member of the lily family. Its underground bulbs come in many shapes, colours, and flavours. This versatile vegetable is a favourite in kitchens around the world.

Growing Onions

FOR SEEDING OR AS SETS

Spacing	Amount	Planting dates
• rows: 2 feet apart	• per person: 30 feet of row	• outdoor: April 15 - May 20
• plants: 2 inches apart	• per 100 feet of row: 2 quarts of sets (bulbs) or 1/2 ounce of seeds	• Seedlings emerge in 8 - 10 days
• depth: 1/2 inch		• Expected crop: 600 bulbs per 100 feet of row

Two plantings per season are possible.
   For early bulbs and green onions, sets are favoured over seed
   No expected yield date is given since green onions can be pulled almost as soon as they appear through the soil. Once they grow larger they can be used as regular onions.

FOR TRANSPLANTING

Spacing	Amount	Planting dates
• rows: 2 feet apart	• per person: 15 feet of row, 1/2 packet of seeds	• indoor: March 10 - April 1
• plants: 4 inches apart	• per 100 feet of row: 2 packets of seeds	• transplanting dates: April 1 - May 10
		• Seedlings emerge in 7 - 10 days
		• Yield in 115 - 135 days
		• Expected crop: 300 bulbs per 100 feet of row

One planting only per season is possible.
   Transplanting is generally confined to late, mild varieties which take in such types as Sweet Spanish strains, Early Harvest, and Calred.

Cooking Onions

green onions: 6 small, less tops = 23 calories
cooking onions: 1 raw: (2-1/2" diameter) = 49 calories

BASIC PREPARATION

Peel under running water to avoid tears. Onions peel easier when they have stood in boiling water for a few minutes.

To chop
Cut in half crosswise. Cube the top cut surface, then cut onion crosswise to release cubes.

To cut onion rings, cut onion crosswise and separate rings.

Note: Remove onion odour from knives by rubbing with a raw potato. Remove odour from hands by rubbing with salt, lemon, or celery salt.

To cook whole
Drop peeled onions into boiling salted water, and cook 20 - 30 minutes or until onions are transparent and can easily be pierced with a fork. Cook sliced onions in the same way but for a shorter time. Drain, season, and add butter.

To roast
Dry onions well, roll in hot fat and cook in a 350°F. oven 1 to 1-1/2 hours.

To bake
Place in a dish with a little butter, milk, and seasoning. Cook in 350°F. oven until tender, 1-1/2 hours.

To French fry
Separate onion slices into rings; dip into flour. Blend eggs and milk. Dip onion rings into mixture and then roll in cracker crumbs. Fry in 365°F. deep fat for 2 - 3 minutes until golden brown. Drain on absorbent paper.

EASY ONIONS AU GRATIN/serves 6

1-1/2 pounds onions, parboiled 2-1/2 cups cheese sauce (p. 126) 1 cup grated cheese 1 tablespoon butter or margarine	Arrange heated onions in shallow buttered casserole. Add cheese sauce. Sprinkle on grated cheese and dot with butter. Broil until heated thoroughly.

ONIONS WITH TOMATO SAUCE/serves 6

18 small onions, peeled and cooked 1/4 teaspoon pepper 1/2 tablespoon butter or margarine 1 tablespoon cooking oil 1 10-ounce can condensed tomato soup 1 cup beef or chicken bouillon	Place all ingredients in 1-1/2-quart casserole. Cover and bake in 375°F. oven 30 minutes.

PARTY SHERRY ONIONS/serves 6

4 onions, peeled, sliced and
    separated into rings
1/3 cup butter or margarine
1/2 teaspoon salt
1/2 teaspoon pepper
3/4 teaspoon oregano
3/4 cup sherry

Sauté onion rings in butter until tender.
Season, add sherry and simmer 3 - 5
minutes.

GOURMET STUFFED BERMUDA ONIONS/serves 6

6 Bermuda onions
1 pound chicken livers, cooked
1 cup mushrooms, quartered
1/2 cup cubed cooked ham
1 garlic clove, finely chopped
    salt, pepper
3 bacon strips, halved
1 cup bouillon

Remove and chop centres of onions.
Blend chopped centres thoroughly with
next four ingredients until quite smooth.
Season and stuff mixture into onions.
Place a piece of bacon on top of each
onion and place in casserole. Cover with
bouillon. Bake in 275°F. oven 1-1/4 hours.

EASY WINTER SALAD/serves 6

2 large Bermuda or Spanish
    onions, sliced
1 cup milk
3 celery hearts
2 large cooked beets
2 hard-cooked eggs
1 teaspoon dry mustard
3/4 teaspoon salt
1/4 teaspoon pepper
1/2 teaspoon sugar
1 teaspoon anchovy paste
    (optional)
1/4 cup olive oil
2 tablespoons wine vinegar

Boil the onions in half milk and half water
until tender. Drain and chill. Slice the celery and beets, and chill while making the
dressing. Chop the eggs, and mix with
mustard, salt, pepper, and sugar. Add
anchovy paste if you wish. Stir in oil,
blending well, and then add vinegar. Mix
the sliced onions with celery and beets,
and pour the dressing over. Let stand
several hours before serving.

ORANGE ONION SALAD/serves 6

6 oranges
1 large sweet onion, sliced thin
1/2 cup French dressing (p. 131)
    few strips of pimiento
    salad greens

Peel and slice the oranges and combine
with the onion. Marinate for about one
hour in the French dressing. Garnish
with pimiento and serve on crisp salad
greens.

Parsley

High in food value, parsley should be eaten as well as used as a colourful garnish or decoration. Enough to supply your needs could be grown in a flowerpot in a sunny window.

Growing Parsley

Spacing	Amount	Planting dates
• rows: 2 feet apart • plants: 4 inches apart • depth: 1/4 inch	• per person: 5 feet of row, 1 packet of seeds	• indoor: March 10 - April 1 • transplanting dates: April 15 - August 1 • outdoor: April 15 - May 15 • Seedlings emerge in 15 - 20 days • Yield in 80+ days • Expected crop: 15 - 25 bunches per 5 feet of row

Three plantings per season are possible.
Parsley can be pot-grown in a sunny window either from seed or transplant.

Cooking Parsley
1 tablespoon, chopped = 1 calorie

BASIC PREPARATION

Chopped fresh or dried, parsley is used to flavour soups, meats, fish, sauces, eggs, breads, butter, marinades and most vegetables and salads.

To chop
Hold stems of several sprigs together; pinch tightly and cut across with a sharp knife or scissors. Discard stems.

To dry
Cut clusters from stems and plunge into boiling water for 30 seconds. Drain. Spread on heavy-duty foil with holes throughout and place in 300°F. oven (door open) until crisp. Store in an airtight container.

To fry
Wash sprigs of parsley and dry well. Fry in 375°F. fat a few seconds, drain and season.

Parsnips

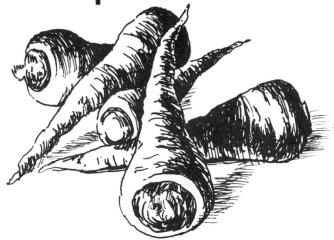

A pale-yellow edible root, parsnip is a member of the umbeliferous family which includes carrot, celery, parsley, fennel, and others.

Growing Parsnips

Spacing	Amount	Planting dates
• rows: 2 feet apart • plants: 4 inches apart • depth: 1/2 inch	• per person: 15 feet of row, 1 packet of seeds • per 100 feet of row: 1/2 ounce of seeds	• outdoor: April 20 - May 20 • Seedlings emerge in 15 - 20 days • Yield in 110 days • Expected crop: 300 roots per 100 feet of row

Only one planting per season is possible. Fresh seed must be used each year.

Cooking Parsnips
1 cup (5 ounces) cooked and drained = 94 calories
2/3 cup (4 ounces) raw = 94 calories

BASIC PREPARATION

Scrub, scrape or pare parsnips. Leave whole or cut into strips, slices, or cubes.

To boil
Cook parsnips in a half to one inch of boiling salted water until tender. Drain and serve with melted butter. Add a little sugar to improve the flavour. Whole parsnips require 25 minutes; slices or cubes 10 - 15 minutes.

To bake
Place sliced parsnips in a covered casserole in 350°F. oven for 30 - 40 minutes. Mash and serve seasoned with grated orange rind.

To fry
Peel parsnips, and cut into fingers or slices. Cook steadily for about 15 minutes in boiling salted water. Drain, coat with batter, or toss in seasoned flour. Put into hot fat and cook until golden brown.

To roast
Roast parsnips in hot fat in the oven for 1-1/4 - 1-1/2 hours.

or

Boil 15 minutes in salted water. Drain, pat dry and then roast in the oven for one hour.

HONEYED PARSNIPS/serves 6

3 tablespoons butter or margarine
4 tablespoons honey
6 medium parsnips, peeled, cut
    into 1-1/2 inch pieces and
    cooked until tender-crisp
cinnamon

Melt butter. Add honey and heat until bubbly. Stir in parsnips. Cover and cook slowly for 5 minutes. Sprinkle with cinnamon.

PARSNIP STEW/serves 6

1/2 cup diced salt pork
3 cups diced parsnips, cooked,
    undrained
1-1/2 cups sliced, cooked potatoes,
    undrained
4 cups warm milk
2 tablespoons flour

1/2 teaspoon salt
1/4 teaspoon pepper

Brown salt pork. Add to vegetables with milk. Bring to boil and thicken with flour paste. Season and serve on toast.

PARSNIP CROQUETTES

Peel, dice parsnips. Cook until tender in boiling salted water. Sieve or mash thoroughly. Add to each pound of parsnip purée, one egg yolk, 1 tablespoon butter, salt, pepper, and a tablespoon milk. Form into croquettes, roll in egg white and crumbs and fry until crisp and golden brown.

PARSNIP FRITTERS

Cook scrubbed parsnips in boiling salted water. Plunge into cold water. Remove skins. Mash pulp; season to taste with salt, pepper, sugar, and spices. Shape into small cakes (use flour to prevent sticking). Sauté on both sides in butter or margarine until delicately browned.

Peas

One of the earliest crops, fresh peas can be enjoyed before many other vegetables early in the growing season.

Growing Peas

Spacing	Amount	Planting dates
• rows: 2 feet apart • plants: 1 inch apart • depth: 1 inch	• per person: 30 feet of row, 1/4 pound of seeds • per 100 feet of row: 1 pound of seeds	• outdoor: March 15 - April 1 • Seedlings emerge in 7 - 10 days • Yield in 60 - 75 days • Expected crop: 25 - 50 quarts per 100 feet of row

Two to three plantings per season are possible.
As peas do not grow best in summer heat, they should be sown early.

Cooking Peas
1/2 cup (2-1/2 ounces) raw = 74 calories

BASIC PREPARATION

Shell peas just before cooking. Cook covered in one inch of boiling salted water for 8 - 12 minutes. (Drop a few pods in the cooking water for extra flavour.)

HERBED PEAS AND CORN/serves 6

3 cups cooked peas 2 cups cooked kernel corn 1/2 cup water (from cooking the peas) 2 tablespoons chopped parsley 1/2 teaspoon oregano 1 tablespoon butter or margarine salt, pepper	*Blend all ingredients together. Heat and serve.*

PEAS AND ONIONS/serves 6

2 tablespoons butter or margarine
2 tablespoons water
1 clove garlic
6 small white onions
3 lettuce leaves, quartered
1 teaspoon sugar
1/4 teaspoon salt
1/8 teaspoon pepper
2-1/2 cups fresh peas or 2 cups frozen peas

Melt butter in a saucepan. Add next 7 ingredients and cover. Simmer for 30 minutes or until onions are almost tender. Add peas. Cover and cook slowly 10 more minutes. Remove garlic and serve.

TUNA, PEAS, AND RICE/serves 6

1 onion, chopped
3 tablespoons butter or margarine
3 cups cooked peas, hot
3 cups cooked rice, hot
1 7-ounce can tuna

1-1/2 teaspoon salt
1/4 teaspoon pepper
1/4 cup grated Parmesan cheese

Sauté onion in butter until golden. Add next six ingredients. Heat thoroughly and serve with cheese.

MUSHROOM-PIMIENTO PEAS/serves 6

3 cups shelled peas, cooked
5 tablespoons butter or margarine
2 4-ounce cans drained, sliced mushrooms
3 canned pimientos, chopped

Mix all ingredients together. Place in 1-1/2 quart casserole. Cover and bake 30 minutes in 325°F. oven.

PEAS AND ASPARAGUS IN ASPIC/serves 6

1 envelope gelatin
1 chicken bouillon cube or 3/4 cup broth
1/3 cup tomato juice
12 cooked asparagus tips
1 cup cooked peas
lettuce
3/4 cup mayonnaise or French dressing (p. 131)

Soften gelatin in 1/4 cup cold water. Heat bouillon cube in 3/4 cup water and pour over gelatin to dissolve. Add broth. Add tomato juice. Pour into mold to depth of 1/4 inch only. When set, arrange the asparagus tips and chill. Chill remaining gelatin until syrupy. Fold in the peas and add to mold. Chill. Serve on lettuce with mayonnaise or French dressing.

CHILLED SOUR CREAM AND GREEN PEAS/serves 6

2-1/2 cups fresh peas or 2 cups frozen peas, cooked and drained
2 tart, red-skinned apples cored, chopped
3 green onions, thinly sliced
1/2 cup sour cream
1 teaspoon horseradish
1/4 teaspoon salt

1/8 teaspoon pepper
2 teaspoons lemon juice
salad greens

Combine first 3 ingredients. Combine next five ingredients and add to vegetables. Chill. Serve in a bowl lined with salad greens.

Peppers

Peppers come in many sizes, shapes and with varying degrees of sweetness.

Sweet peppers are eaten raw or cooked.

Hot peppers are used in cooking, pickled or dried.

The condiments, paprika, chili powder, cayenne, red pepper and crushed red peppers, are all made from dried and ground pepper of varying degrees of pungency.

Growing Peppers

Spacing	Amount	Planting dates
• rows: 2 feet apart • plants: 2 feet apart • depth: 1/2 inch	• per person: 15 feet of row, 1/4 packet of seeds • per 100 feet of row: 1 packet of seeds	• indoor: March 15 - April 1 • transplanting date: June 1 • Seedlings emerge in 10 - 14 days • Yield in 65 - 75 days • Expected crop: 300 fruit per 100 feet of row

Peppers should be planted in a rich, warm soil in an area of the garden where there is protection from the prevailing wind.

Cooking Peppers

green pepper, raw, 3-1/2 ounces = 22 calories
                    cooked, 3-1/2 ounces = 18 calories
red pepper, raw, 3-1/2 ounces = 31 calories
pimiento, canned (solids and liquid), 3-1/2 ounces = 27 calories

BASIC PREPARATION

Wash pepper. Remove tops, seeds, and ribs. Leave whole, or cut in halves, strips, rings, or dice.

To stuff and bake
Cook peppers for 5 minutes in boiling salted water. Drain, stuff, and bake in 375°F. oven 25 - 30 minutes.

To pickle
Pack peppers whole in a hot sterilized jar. Add 1 teaspoon salt and 1 clove garlic. Cover with boiling vinegar. Seal jar and let stand in refrigerator for 2 weeks before using.

Use chopped peppers as condiments, in cocktail dips, devilled eggs or sandwich fillings.

The vinegar in which they have been pickled can be used where a hot effect is desired.

To roast
Place peppers in broiler under flame until blistered on all sides. Place in a paper bag and steam in oven for 20 - 30 minutes. Remove stems and seeds, and cut pepper into strips. Add oil, vinegar, salt, and pepper, and chill 3 - 4 hours.

PEPERADE/serves 6

1-1/2 cups sweet peppers, sliced	*Sauté peppers and onion in butter until*
1-1/2 cups onions, sliced	*tender. Add eggs and seasoning. Chill*
2 tablespoons butter	*and serve as a condiment.*
2 hard-cooked eggs, chopped	
seasoning	

RED AND GREEN PEPPERS WITH MUSHROOMS/serves 6

3/4 pound mushrooms, thickly sliced, sautéed	*Combine all ingredients. Bring to boil for 1 - 2 minutes. Serve.*
1/2 teaspoon pepper	
3 tablespoons butter or margarine	
1 teaspoon salt	
1 green pepper cut into six pieces	
1 red pepper cut into six pieces	

ITALIAN STUFFED GREEN PEPPERS/serves 6

6 green peppers, remove tops and seeds	6 1-inch cubes Mozzarella
1 28-ounce can tomatoes, drained (reserve liquid)	2 tablespoons olive or salad oil
4 cups large bread cubes	2 tablespoons butter or margarine
4 ripe olives, chopped	1/4 cup flour
4 capers (optional)	
1/2 cup grated Parmesan cheese	*Mix 1/2 can tomatoes with next 9 ingre-*
2 tablespoons chopped parsley	*dients. Stuff peppers with this mixture*
1/2 teaspoon salt	*and top with a cube of cheese. Place in*
1/8 teaspoon pepper	*1-1/2-quart casserole and pour over rest*
1/2 clove garlic, finely chopped	*of tomatoes with juice. Cover and bake at*
1/2 teaspoon oregano	*375°F. oven 40 minutes. Thicken gravy*
	with oil, butter, and flour, and serve over
	peppers.

Potatoes

Potatoes were first grown by the Indians in the mountainous country of South America. Ireland once based its economy on this popular vegetable, much as Holland did on its tulip bulbs. Now a North American staple, potatoes are available in many forms and used for many purposes.

Growing Potatoes

Spacing	Amount	Planting dates
• rows: 3 feet apart	• per person: 30 feet of row, 3 pounds (30 eyes)	• indoor sprouting: April 1 - April 10
• plants: 1 foot apart	• per 100 feet of row: 10 pounds of seeds	• transplant sprouts: May 1 - May 14
• depth: 4 inches		• Seedlings emerge in 8 - 12 days
		• Expected crop: 150 pounds per 100 feet of row

Note: There are three types of potatoes: extra-early, early, and late. Check with a local authority about which types thrive best in your locality.

Two plantings per season are possible.
The application of a complete fertilizer is recommended.

Cooking Potatoes

baked, 1 medium = 97 calories
boiled, peeled, diced, 1 cup (4 ounces) = 105 calories
boiled, unpeeled, 1 medium (5 ounces) = 118 calories
chips, ten 2" diameter (2/3 ounce) = 108 calories
French fried, 8 pieces (1-1/3 ounces) = 157 calories
fried, 1 cup (5-2/3 ounces) = 479 calories
hash browned, 1 cup (6-1/2 ounces) = 470 calories
mashed with milk, 1/2 cup (3-1/3 ounces) =78 calories
mashed with milk and butter, 1/2 cup (3-1/3 ounces) = 120 calories
steamed, diced, 1 cup or 1 medium (4 ounces) = 105 calories

BASIC PREPARATION

Scrub thoroughly. For best food value, leave skins on. If skins are removed, keep peelings as thin as possible.

To boil
Cook, covered, in boiling salted water until tender. Whole potatoes—30 - 35 minutes, small or sliced potatoes—20 - 25 minutes.

To bake
Scrub potatoes and dry. For soft skins, rub with a little butter or oil. Place in oven at 450°F. 45 - 60 minutes. Test with a fork to see if they are cooked. Cut a small cross on the top, hold in both hands and squeeze gently until the cross opens in four points. Stuff if desired.

Stuffing variations
1. Strips of anchovy topped with an olive.
2. Bacon skewered around potato with a cocktail stick.
3. Fried egg with tomato slices and chopped chives.
4. Chopped fried mushrooms garnished with a strip of bacon rolled up and secured with a cocktail stick.
5. Peas mixed with potato flesh, garnished with butter.
6. A grilled kidney garnished with fried onion rings.
7. Cooked chopped meat, garnished with parsley.
8. Sultanas and cubes of cheese.

Garnishes for baked potatoes
1. Sour cream
2. Whipped butter
3. Chopped green onion or chives
4. Minced parsley
5. Caraway seeds
6. Chopped dill
7. Grated Gruyere cheese
8. Grated Cheddar cheese
9. Slivers of red onion
10. Seasoned salt and pepper
11. Minced red and green peppers
12. Sliced stuffed olives
13. Crumbled fried bacon or salt pork
14. Toasted sesame seeds

To pan roast

Peel and boil potatoes for 10 minutes. Drain, arrange in roasting pan or shallow casserole, and brush with meat drippings or other fat. Bake in 400°F. oven 45 minutes. Turn occasionally and brush often.

or

Place parboiled potatoes around roast and bake during last hour of roasting (325°F.).

To French fry

Peel potatoes. Cut in half-inch slices and then into strips. Rinse in cold water and dry. Place in hot fat 325 - 350°F. until tender and brown. Drain and serve.

QUICK 'N' EASY SCALLOPED POTATOES/serves 6

6 potatoes, peeled, thinly sliced
  salt, pepper
1 can condensed mushroom soup
1 cup milk
  butter
  fresh chives or a little onion,
    chopped
	Arrange potatoes in casserole or dish. Season well. Mix together soup and milk, and pour over potatoes. Add a little butter. Bake for approximately 2 hours in 350°F. oven. Garnish with chopped chives or onion.

BAKED HERBED POTATOES/serves 6

8 cups diced potatoes, partially cooked 1 onion, minced 1 cup celery and leaves, chopped 1/3 cup melted butter or margarine 1/4 cup parsley, minced 1 teaspoon salt 1/4 teaspoon pepper 1 teaspoon poultry seasoning	Mix all ingredients in shallow casserole. Bake in 375°F. oven 30 minutes.

POTATO APPLE SALAD/serves 6

1 pound potatoes, boiled in jackets 1 pound apples 2 tablespoons olive oil 3 tablespoons vinegar 1/2 teaspoon salt 1/8 teaspoon pepper 2 hard-cooked eggs 2 cooked beets, diced (garnish)	Peel and dice potatoes. Core, peel and dice apples. Make the dressing by mixing oil, vinegar, salt and pepper. Pour this over mixture of potatoes and apples, and garnish with sliced eggs and/or beets.

POTATO SALAD/serves 4 - 6

2 pounds potatoes, boiled in jackets 6 tablespoons olive oil 6 tablespoons wine vinegar 1/2 cup beef broth 3/4 teaspoon salt 1/4 teaspoon pepper 1 onion, minced 1 tablespoon minced parsley	Peel and slice potatoes while warm. Pour mixture of oil, vinegar, and broth over the potatoes while they are still warm. Let stand for one hour. Mix salt, pepper, onions, and parsley, and fold into salad.

POTATO APPETIZER/makes 36 plus

3 potatoes, cooked in jackets,
    not too soft
2 tablespoons commercial sour
    cream
1/2 cup mayonnaise
1/8 teaspoon curry
    salt, pepper

Peel cooled potatoes, and cut into small cubes. Mix remaining ingredients and coat each potato cube. Serve with toothpicks.

CURRIED POTATO SOUP/serves 6

3 cups diced raw potatoes
2-1/2 cups boiling water
3 chicken or beef bouillon cubes
1/2 teaspoon salt
1 garlic clove, minced
1-3/4 teaspoons curry powder
1 small onion, chopped
2 cups milk
2 tablespoons butter or margarine
1/4 teaspoon pepper

Combine first 7 ingredients. Cover and cook until potatoes are tender. Remove from heat and mash potatoes in the liquid. Add milk, butter, and pepper. Reheat.

SALT PORK AND POTATO CHOWDER/serves 4

1/4 pound salt pork, minced
1 large onion, chopped
1/2 cup finely diced celery and leaves
3 cups diced, cooked potatoes
3 cups water
3 cups milk
    salt, pepper
8 saltine crackers, crumbled

Fry salt pork in saucepan until golden brown. Remove from pan. Add onion, celery and potatoes to pan. Cover and cook for 10 minutes. Stir occasionally. Add water. Cover and simmer 15 minutes. Add milk and heat. Season with salt and pepper. Before serving add pork and crumbled crackers.

POTATO SOUP PARMENTIER/serves 6

3 green onions, chopped
    butter
4 medium potatoes, peeled, diced
    salt
1 cup milk, brought to a boil
1 egg yolk, beaten
    white bread, cut into squares, and
    browned in butter

Sauté onions in butter. Place potatoes in salted water to cover. Add onions. Cover and cook slowly until tender. Pass entire mixture through food chopper. Add milk and enough water to make soup the right consistency. Bring to boil. Remove from heat. Add small amount of soup to egg, stirring constantly. Pour mixture into soup. Mix well and pour into serving bowls. Add 1 tablespoon butter and the bread squares and serve.

GREEK STYLE POTATO SOUP

To 1 quart Potato Soup Parmentier, add 2 or 3 cooked or canned tomatoes and 1/2 cup cooked rice. Serve with a sprinkling of parsley.

Pumpkins

Since it requires a lot of growing space, pumpkin may not be a good crop for the small garden—except perhaps to grow one's own jack-o'-lantern.

Growing Pumpkins

Spacing	Amount	Planting dates
Bush	• per person: 5 feet of row, 1 packet of seeds	• indoor: April 15 - April 20 (in peat pots)
• rows: 4 - 6 feet apart		• transplanting date: June 1
• plants: thinned to 18 - 24 inches apart	• per 100 feet of row: 2 ounces of seeds	• outdoor: May 20 - May 31
• depth: 1 inch		• Seedlings emerge in 7 - 12 days
Vining		• Yield in 100 - 110 days
• rows: 6 - 8 feet apart		• Expected crop: 22 fruit per 100 feet of row
• plants: 1 - 2 feet apart		
• depth: 1 inch		

Two plantings per season are possible.
Apply plenty of organic matter (preferably manure) to the trench in which the pumpkin seed is sown.

Cooking Pumpkins
3-1/2 ounces, raw = 26 calories
3-1/2 ounces, canned = 33 calories

BASIC PREPARATION
Select pumpkins that are fairly firm of rind, a bright-orange colour, heavy for their size, and free of blemishes. Three pounds of fresh pumpkin equals three cups cooked and mashed.

To store
Pantry shelf, whole - 1 month
Refrigerator, whole - 1 to 4 months.
Prepared and frozen - 1 year.

To boil
Cut the pumpkin and remove seeds. Cut into small pieces and peel. Cook in boiling salted water 25 to 30 minutes. Drain. Mash or force through a food mill. Use for making pies or other desserts. Or reheat, season with butter, salt, pepper, and serve as a vegetable.

To bake
Prepare as for boiling. Place in a shallow oven dish. Brush with butter or margarine and sprinkle with salt and pepper. Bake uncovered in 350°F. oven 45 to 50 minutes. Serve as a vegetable.

To steam
Do not peel. Steam in large steamer or colander for 50 minutes. Scrape out cooked pulp. Mash, and use for dessert or as vegetable.

To freeze
Boil or steam pumpkin as described. Mash, cool, spoon into a freezer container leaving 1/2-inch head space, and seal.

FLUFFY PUMPKIN PIE/serves 8

1 3-ounce package apple- or orange-flavoured jelly powder
1/4 cup boiling water
1/2 cup brown sugar
1-1/2 cups cooked, mashed pumpkin
1/2 teaspoon salt
1 teaspoon vanilla
2 teaspoons mixed pumpkin pie spice
1 cup low calorie, whipped dessert topping
1 baked 9-inch pie shell

Mix jelly powder with water. Stir until dissolved. Add next 5 ingredients. Chill until thickened. Fold in whipped dessert topping. Pour into prepared pastry shell. Chill until set.

CREAMY PUMPKIN TARTS/serves 8

2 cups cooked mashed or canned pumpkin
1/2 teaspoon salt
3/4 teaspoon pumpkin pie spice
1 tablespoon fancy molasses
1 cup skim milk
1 package vanilla, butterscotch, or caramel pudding, (cooked type)
1/3 cup brown sugar
8 large baked tart shells

Heat the first 4 ingredients in top of double boiler. Stir in milk mixed with pudding powder and sugar. Cook and stir until thickened. Spoon into baked tart shells; cool. Cover with whipped topping if you wish.

Radishes

Radishes are the pungent fleshy root of a hardy plant. They come in many shapes and colours, and their taste varies from mild to peppery. The common radish is an annual, but the so-called winter radishes, such as China Rose, White Chinese, and Black Spanish, are biennials. They grow more slowly and produce larger roots, which can be stored much longer than the other varieties.

Growing Radishes

Spacing	Amount	Planting dates
• rows: 1 foot apart	• per person: 5 feet of row, 1/2 packet of seeds	• outdoor: April 20 - August 1
• plants: 1 inch apart		• Seedlings emerge in 3 - 6 days
• depth: 1/2 inch	• per 100 feet of row: 1 ounce of seeds	• Yield in 25 - 38 days
		• Expected crop: 1,200 roots per 100 feet of row

Four plantings per season are possible.
Radishes will continue to grow until the snow begins to fall.

Cooking Radishes
3-1/2 ounces, raw = 17 calories

BASIC PREPARATION

Remove leaves and rootlets and wash radishes thoroughly. They can be refrigerated up to one week, but *do not freeze.*

Before using wash again and be sure all leaves and rootlets have been removed. Radishes may be cut in attractive ways on a relish plate or to garnish salads.

Rhubarb

The stalks of the rhubarb plant are used in many popular desserts. Rhubarb is a perennial vegetable. Since it stays in the same place year after year, it requires good, rich topsoil.

Growing Rhubarb

Spacing	Amount	Planting dates
• rows: 4 feet apart • plants: 4 feet apart	• per person: 15 feet of row, 4 roots • per 100 feet of row: 25 roots	• outdoor: April 20 - May 20 • Yield in 2 - 3 years • Expected crop: 300 stalks per 100 feet of row

Cooking Rhubarb
3-1/2 ounces, cooked with added sugar = 141 calories

BASIC PREPARATION

When picking or purchasing rhubarb, look for fresh, firm, large stalks with a bright dark red or cherry colour. When purchasing, remember that one pound equals 2 cups cooked.

To store
It is best to use rhubarb as soon as possible. If it is stored, it will keep for the following lengths of time:

Fresh, unrefrigerated: uncooked—1 - 3 days
Fresh, refrigerated: cooked—4 - 5 days
Fresh, frozen: in frozen food compartment—2 - 3 days
in freezer—1 year
Canned on pantry shelf—1 year

To prepare
Wash. Remove leaves and stem ends. If tender, do not peel. Cut stalks into inch-long pieces. Add only enough water to cover. Cook until tender. Stir in sugar to taste. Serve warm or chilled.

BAKED ROSY RHUBARB/serves 4

1 pound fresh rhubarb
1 cup sugar
1/2 cup water

Cut rhubarb into one-inch pieces. Place in shallow casserole with sugar and water. Bake in 350°F. oven for 35 minutes. Chill before serving.

RHUBARB TANGY FRESH APPLESAUCE

Diced fresh rhubarb added to apples when making fresh applesauce gives a rosy colour and tangy flavour.

RHUBARB DELUXE/serves 4

1-1/2 pounds rhubarb
1-1/2 cups water
1/2 cup sugar
1/2 teaspoon vanilla extract
2-1/2 tablespoons cornstarch
heavy cream

Cut rhubarb into 1/2-inch slices. Add water and sugar and simmer until mushy. Add vanilla. Mix cornstarch with a little cold water; stir into rhubarb. Cook stirring constantly for five minutes, or until thickened. Serve warm or chilled with cream, a little extra sugar if desired, and butter cookies.

RHUBARB AND STRAWBERRY PIE

pastry for 2-crust 9-inch pie, unbaked
3/4 cup sugar
1/4 cup all purpose flour
2 cups diced rhubarb
1 pint strawberries, hulled
2 tablespoons butter or margarine

Roll a little more than half of pastry 1/8 inch thick and line 9-inch pie pan. Mix sugar and flour, and sprinkle a small amount in pastry lined pan. Combine remaining sugar mixture with rhubarb and berries. Put in pie pan and dot with butter. Roll remaining pastry 1/8 inch thick. Put on pie, trim edges and flute. Cut a few slits for steam to escape. Bake in 425°F. oven for 40 to 50 minutes.

Rutabagas and Turnips

Rutabagas and turnips are similar cool-season vegetables, although rutabaga roots require more time to develop than turnips. There are other differences as well. With turnips, white-fleshed varieties are most commonly grown, but with rutabaga, yellow-fleshed varieties are preferred. Turnips can be stored for several weeks at low temperature, but rutabagas can be stored for a much longer time.

Only the root of the rutabaga is consumed. However, turnip tops are often eaten as a green. Turnip roots are usually served as a boiled vegetable.

Growing Rutabagas

Spacing	Amount	Planting dates
• rows: 30 inches apart	• per person: 10 feet of row, 1/4 packet of seeds	• outdoor: July 1 - July 15
• plants: thinned to 4 - 8 inches apart	• per 100 feet of row: 1 packet of seeds	• Seedlings emerge in 5 - 10 days
		• Yield in 90 - 100 days
		• Expected crop: 200 roots per 100 feet of row

Growing Turnips

Spacing	Amount	Planting dates
• rows: 14 - 18 inches apart • plants: 2 - 3 inches apart	• per person: 10 feet of row, 1/4 packet of seeds • per 100 feet of row: 1 packet of seeds	• outdoor: July 15 - August 1 • Seedlings emerge in 5 -10 days • Yield in 50 - 100 days • Expected crop: 500 roots per 100 feet of row

Only one planting per season is possible for both turnips and rutabagas. Both do best as a fall crop.

Cooking Rutabagas and Turnips
3/4 cup, raw = 45 calories

BASIC PREPARATION

Wash, pare, and slice or dice.

Cook, covered, in one inch of boiling salted water until tender, 12 - 15 minutes. Drain, season, and serve with melted butter or margarine.

Sliced turnips may be seasoned and baked in a covered casserole in a 375°F. oven 45 minutes.

MASHED RUTABAGAS

Boil rutabagas, drain and mash. Add butter, a little grated nutmeg and milk or cream. Blend well.

GLAZED RUTABAGAS

Choose very small rutabagas. Peel and slice. Cook in boiling salted water until tender and drain. Cover with a little sugar blended with vegetable water. Heat in 350°F. oven until rutabagas are golden brown and liquids are absorbed.

SPICY RUTABAGA PIE

1-1/2 cups cooked rutabaga
1 cup brown sugar, firmly packed
2 tablespoons table molasses
2 eggs, beaten lightly
1-1/4 cups undiluted evaporated milk, or light cream
1/2 teaspoon ground ginger
1 teaspoon cinnamon
1/2 teaspoon nutmeg or mace
1/2 teaspoon cloves
1/2 teaspoon salt
1 teaspoon vanilla

1 unbaked, deep 9-inch pie shell
whipped cream
sliced filberts

Beat first 11 ingredients together until thoroughly blended. Pour into unbaked pastry shell. Bake in 450°F. oven for 15 minutes. Reduce heat to 350°F. and continue baking about 40 minutes, or until filling is almost set (until a knife inserted in centre comes out clean). Do not overbake. Cool and top with whipped cream and sliced filberts.

RUTABAGAS AND LEMON BUTTER/serves 6

3 cups pared rutabaga cubes,
   cooked
3 tablespoons butter or
   margarine
1-1/2 tablespoons lemon juice
2 tablespoons chopped parsley
   paprika

Shake drained rutabagas over heat to dry. Melt butter, add lemon juice and parsley, and pour over rutabaga. Garnish with paprika.

EASY RUTABAGA SCALLOP/serves 6

1 cup water
1 cup milk
3/4 teaspoon salt
4 cups thinly sliced rutabaga
2 cups pared sliced carrots
1/2 cup sliced onion
1/4 cup diced celery
1/4 cup diced green pepper
1 tablespoon butter or margarine
1 cup grated Cheddar cheese
5 tablespoons breadcrumbs

Boil together water and milk. Add next six ingredients, cover and simmer until tender (20 minutes). Add remaining ingredients. Cover and heat until cheese is melted.

RUTABAGA 'N' SOUR CREAM/serves 6

2 pounds fresh rutabaga, peeled,
   cooked, mashed
1/4 teaspoon salt
1/2 teaspoon celery salt
1 cup sour cream
1/4 teaspoon ground ginger
1/8 teaspoon pepper

Season mashed rutabaga with remaining ingredients. Serve hot.

TURNIP RING/serves 4 - 6

3 tablespoons all-purpose flour
2 tablespoons light brown sugar
2 tablespoons hot bacon fat
1 cup milk
4 egg yolks, beaten
2 cups cooked, mashed turnip or
   rutabaga
   salt and pepper
4 egg whites, beaten until stiff
   parsley

Stir flour and sugar into bacon fat, then gradually stir in milk. Cook, stirring constantly, until smooth and thickened. Remove from heat. Gradually stir into egg yolks. Add turnip and seasonings. Fold in beaten egg whites, and turn into a well-greased 1-1/2 quart mold. Bake in 375°F. oven 30 - 35 minutes. Remove from oven, cover with a towel for 5 minutes. Unmold and garnish with parsley.

FLUFFY TURNIPS/serves 6

2 pounds fresh turnip or rutabaga
   pared and cubed
1 10-1/2 ounce can beef consommé
1/2 teaspoon sugar
2 teaspoons onion, chopped
2 tablespoons parsley, chopped

Cook turnips in consommé for 12 - 15 minutes. Mash in liquid until fluffy. Add remaining ingredients. Reheat and serve.

Spinach

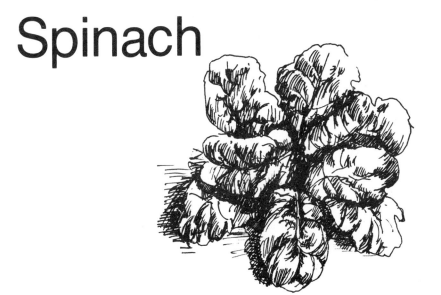

Spinach is an annual herb that originated in southwestern Asia. It is grown for its green leaves.

Growing Spinach

Spinach does not grow well in hot sandy soil. It thrives in a rich loam under cool conditions.

FOR EARLY SOWING

Spacing	Amount	Planting dates
• rows: 12 - 18 inches apart • plants: 6 inches apart • depth: 3/4 inch	• per person: 15 feet of row, 1 packet of seeds • per 100 feet of row: 1 ounce of seeds	• outdoor: April 20 - May 20 • Seedlings emerge in 7 - 12 days • Yield in 40 - 45 days • Expected crop: 200 plants per 100 feet of row

Two plantings per season are possible.

FOR LATE SOWING

Spacing	Amount	Planting dates
• rows: 12 - 18 inches apart • plants: 6 inches apart • depth: 3/4 inch	• per person: 15 feet of row, 1 packet of seeds • per 100 feet of row: 1 ounce of seeds	• outdoor: July 15 - August 10 • Seedlings emerge in 7 - 12 days • Yield in 40 - 45 days • Expected crop: 200 plants per 100 feet of row

Two plantings per season are possible.

Cooking Spinach
4 ounces, raw = 22 calories

BASIC PREPARATION

Rinse well in cold running water. Drain.
 Cook using water remaining on the leaves after washing. Do not add additional water. Cook 5 - 8 minutes, until tender. Drain and season. Use butter or margarine, salt and pepper, fresh lemon juice or nutmeg.

CHOPPED SPINACH

Cook spinach with a little salt until tender. Drain. Chop quickly, and reheat with pepper and butter.

CREAMED SPINACH

Cook spinach with salt until tender, and chop finely. Stir in a thick white sauce *(p. 126), allowing 3/4 cup of sauce for each pound of raw spinach.*

SPINACH SOUFFLÉ

2 tablespoons butter or margarine	*Heat butter. Stir in flour, and cook several*
2 tablespoons flour	*minutes. Add milk, spinach, and season-*
1 pound cooked spinach, finely chopped	*ing. Beat in egg yolks and cheese. Then fold in stiffly beaten egg whites. Pour into*
1/3 cup milk	*soufflé dish and bake in 375°F. oven 30 -*
seasoning	*35 minutes.*
4 eggs, separated	
1/2 cup grated Parmesan cheese (optional)	

SPINACH AND BACON SALAD/serves 6

2 pounds spinach	*Wash spinach thoroughly. Dry and break*
3 hard-cooked eggs, chopped	*in bite-size pieces into salad bowl.*
8 slices crisp cooked bacon, crumbled	*Sprinkle with chopped eggs and bacon. Toss with yogurt dressing or French*
1/4 cup yogurt or French dressing (p. 131)	*dressing.*

SPINACH SALAD/serves 4

1 pound spinach	*Wash spinach several times and re-*
3/4 teaspoon salt	*move hard stems. Cut spinach into strips,*
1 tablespoon sugar	*dry and chill. Make dressing by mixing*
1/2 teaspoon paprika	*the salt, sugar, paprika and mustard with*
1/2 teaspoon dry mustard	*Worcestershire sauce, lemon juice and*
1 teaspoon Worcestershire sauce	*catsup. Slowly add oil and vinegar alter-*
2 tablespoons lemon juice	*nately while beating in an electric mixer*
1/4 cup catsup	*or with a rotary hand mixer. The dressing*
1 cup oil	*should be thick. Stir in a lump of ice to*
2 tablespoons vinegar	*ensure the thickness. Serve over the spinach.*

Squash

There are two main types of squash: summer and winter squash.

Summer squash are small, quick-growing, with thin skins and light-coloured flesh. They are picked before the skin and seeds harden. Common varieties of summer squash are:

Scallop, Pattypan or Cymling: disc-shaped with scalloped edges.
   3-1/2 ounces, boiled and drained = 16 calories
Chayote: pear-shaped, about the size of an acorn.
   3-1/2 ounces, boiled and drained = 14 calories
Yellow Crookneck: curved neck, larger at the top than at the base.
   3-1/2 ounces, boiled and drained = 15 calories
Yellow Straightneck: similar to the Crookneck, with a straight neck and much larger.
Zucchini (sometimes called Italian Marrow): 10 - 12 inches long and a little thicker at one end.
   3-1/2 ounces, boiled and drained = 12 calories
Cocozelle: 6 - 8 inches long, cylindrical, spiral; the skin is ribbed with dark green and yellow stripes.
   3-1/2 ounces, boiled and drained = 12 calories

Winter squash have a hard, coarse, rough rind and are dark green or orange in colour. Common varieties are:

Acorn or Pepper: Acorn shaped, 5 - 8 inches long, and 4 - 5 inches thick with a thin, smooth, dark green ribbed shell which becomes orange during storage.
   3-1/2 ounces, boiled = 34 calories
   3-1/2 ounces, baked = 55 calories
Buttercup: 5 inches long and 6 - 8 inches in diameter with a turbanlike formation at the blossom end. The hard skin is dark green with small grey markings, the stripes are grey and so is the turban formation.
   3-1/2 ounces, boiled = 21 calories
   3-1/2 ounces, baked = 53 calories

Butternut: Cylindrical shape with a bulblike base; 9 - 10 inches long. The smooth hard skin is a light brown or dark yellow.

3-1/2 ounces, boiled = 41 calories
3-1/2 ounces, baked = 68 calories

Hubbard: Globe-shaped with a thick tapered neck and a diameter of 9 - 12 inches. Colour can vary from bronzy green to orange-red, and the skin is hard, ridged, and warted.

3-1/2 ounces, boiled = 30 calories
3-1/2 ounces, baked = 50 calories

Growing Squash

Spacing	Amount	Planting dates
• rows: 8 feet apart • plants: 2 feet apart • depth: 1 inch	• per person: 5 feet of row, 1 packet of seeds • per 100 feet of row: 1 ounce of seeds	• indoor: April 15 - April 20 (in peat pots) • transplanting date: June 1 • outdoor: May 20 - May 31 • Seedlings emerge in 7 - 10 days • Yield in 95 - 100 days • Expected crop: 250 fruit per 100 feet of row

Two plantings per season are possible.
Squash, pumpkin, and vegetable marrow must be dusted for protection against the cucumber beetle.

Cooking Squash

BASIC PREPARATION

Wash well to remove wax coating if necessary. Cut into halves or quarters lengthwise, into rings crosswise, or suitable serving size.

To bake
Place halves, cut side down, in a pan with a half inch of water. Bake in 400°F. oven 40 - 50 minutes. Turn cut side up; season, add butter, a little sugar, minced onion, nutmeg, mace or ginger. Bake until sugar and butter melt.

or

Bake whole, with one or two small pricks through skin, in 400°F. oven for one hour, or until tender. Cut and remove seeds. Season to taste before serving.

To oven-steam
Arrange pieces cut side up, add 1/2 inch water and cover. Bake as before.

To mash
Prepare as for baking. When tender, cool slightly and scrape out pulp. Mash. Season to taste with salt, pepper, butter and brown sugar or other spices. Serve like sweet potatoes.

BAKED SQUASH SUPREME/serves 6

3 acorn squash, halved, cleaned melted butter 3/4 cup heavy cream 3/4 cup maple syrup	Place squash cut side up in greased baking dish. Brush inside of each half with melted butter. Mix together cream and maple syrup and fill each squash cavity. Bake uncovered in 350°F. oven one hour.

SAUSAGE-FILLED ACORN SQUASH/serves 6

3 acorn squash, halved, cleaned 1-1/2 pounds pork sausage meat, cooked, drained 1 onion, finely chopped 2 cups soft breadcrumbs 1 teaspoon salt 1/8 teaspoon pepper 1/8 teaspoon allspice	Place squash halves cut side down in 1/2 inch of water and bake in 400°F. oven 40 - 50 minutes. Blend remaining ingredients and fill centres of tender squash halves. Bake uncovered in 375°F. oven 30 minutes.

GLAZED WHOLE SQUASH/serves 6

1 butternut squash 3/4 cup well-packed dark brown sugar 1/4 cup butter or margarine 1 tablespoon water	Bake whole squash in 350°F. oven one hour. Peel leaving squash whole. Mix remaining ingredients in a saucepan, and simmer 3 - 4 minutes. Spoon over squash, bake in 350°F. oven 15 minutes or until squash is glazed. Cut into serving pieces.

TOP-OF-STOVE SQUASH AU GRATIN/serves 6

5 tablespoons butter or margarine 6 cups thinly sliced squash 2 onions, sliced 1 teaspoon salt 1/8 teaspoon pepper 3 tomatoes, peeled, sliced 3/4 cup grated Cheddar cheese soy sauce (optional)	Melt butter; add next 5 ingredients. Cover and cook 12 - 15 minutes. Sprinkle with cheese and soy sauce.

Cooking Zucchini

BASIC PREPARATION

Wash but do not peel. Remove stem and blossom ends. Cut into half-inch slices or cubes.

Add zucchini to one inch of boiling salted water. Cook, covered, 10 - 15 minutes, or until tender. Drain and season to taste.

Zucchini may also be baked, creamed, or used for fritters. Young zucchini can be sautéed in butter until tender. Season to taste with salt, pepper, and garlic.

SAUTÉED ZUCCHINI/serves 6

1-1/2 pounds zucchini, each 5 or 6
    inches long
  3 tablespoons olive oil
    butter or margarine
  1/2 teaspoon salt
  1/8 teaspoon pepper

Cut zucchini in 1/8-inch thick slices. Heat oil in frying pan and sauté zucchini until lightly browned. Turn to brown evenly. Sprinkle with salt and pepper.

Variations

1. Savoury zucchini: Sauté 1 clove garlic, mashed, in oil. Add zucchini and cook until browned. Add 1 tablespoon chopped parsley, 1 teaspoon oregano and a pinch of sugar with other spices.
2. Crunchy zucchini: Add 1/3 pound chopped walnuts to zucchini while cooking. Garnish with 1/4 cup walnut halves.
3. Sautéed cabbage and zucchini: Sauté 1 coarsely chopped head of cabbage in oil, add 1 thinly sliced onion, cover and simmer 30 minutes. Add zucchini and sauté.

ZUCCHINI VEGETABLE SALAD

  8 zucchini, thinly sliced
  2 tomatoes, peeled and coarsely
    chopped
  1 green pepper, chopped
  1 onion, chopped fine
  1 teaspoon sugar
3/4 teaspoon salt
1/2 teaspoon pepper

1/4 teaspoon paprika
  3 tablespoons mayonnaise or French
    dressing (p. 131)
    lettuce

Mix zucchini with next 7 ingredients. Add dressing a tablespoon at a time. Do not make the salad too moist. Serve on lettuce.

BAKED ZUCCHINI WITH CORN/serves 6

  3 cobs of corn
  3 zucchini thinly sliced
  1 onion, thinly sliced
1/4 cup butter or margarine, melted
1/2 teaspoon salt
1/4 teaspoon pepper
  1 teaspoon chili powder, or to taste
  1 8-ounce can tomato sauce

Grate corn kernels from cobs. Mix with remaining ingredients except sauce. Put in shallow 1-1/2-quart casserole, and pour sauce over top. Bake uncovered in 350°F. oven 45 minutes.

ZUCCHINI FANS/serves 6

  6 medium zucchini
  2 tomatoes, cored
1/4 cup water
  2 tablespoons salad oil
1/4 teaspoon salt
1/4 teaspoon garlic powder

Cut ends from zucchini. Make 3 lengthwise cuts to within one inch of one end, forming a fan. Cut tomatoes into 1/3-inch wedges, and insert between zucchini slices. Place in large frying pan and add remaining ingredients. Simmer for 15 minutes.

Sweet Potatoes

The sweet potato is the enlarged root of a vine of the morning glory family.

Growing Sweet Potatoes

Sweet potatoes require a long frost-free period for growing, and are not suited to northern climates.

Cooking Sweet Potatoes
4 ounces (5" x 2"), baked = 183 calories

BASIC PREPARATION

Select smooth, plump, uniform potatoes. Clean and dry. Scrub and trim bruised or woody potatoes. Cook before peeling.

To boil
Boil covered in salted water 25 - 30 minutes. Drain, remove skins, then mash, candy, or glaze.

To French fry
Boil 10 minutes only. Drain, peel, cut into strips and cook in hot 375°F. deep fat until browned.

To bake
Grease clean skins. Bake potatoes in 400°F. oven 30 - 40 minutes. Peel or serve in skins.

To pan-roast
Peel potatoes and cook in boiling salted water 10 - 12 minutes. Drain and place around roast 1 hour before serving.

To charcoal-broil
Grease clean skins. Wrap potatoes in 2 layers of heavy-duty aluminum foil, and place in coals for 45 minutes.

Swiss Chard

A member of the beet family, chard is not red and not beet-shaped, rather looks like broad-stemmed celery.

Growing Swiss Chard

Spacing	Amount	Planting dates
• rows: 2 feet apart	• per person: 15 feet of row, 1 packet of seeds	• outdoor: May 1 - June 15
• plants: 1 foot apart		• Seedlings emerge in 7 - 10 days
• depth: 1/2 inch	• per 100 feet of row: 1 ounce of seeds	• Yield in 55+ days
		• Expected crop: 100 plants per 100 feet of row

Many plantings are possible per season. Harvest only the outside stalks.

Cooking Swiss Chard
1-1/2 cups (3-1/2 ounces) raw = 24 calories

BASIC PREPARATION

Remove the root ends, and separate leaves and stalks. Cut stalks into 2-inch lengths and chop the leaves.

To cook

Cook in a small quantity of boiling salted water. The stalks require 10 - 15 minutes cooking, and leaves 5 minutes. Therefore, add the leaves to the stalks for last 5 minutes of cooking. Drain, season with salt, pepper, butter or margarine and lemon juice.

or

Sauté stalks in butter 15 - 20 minutes.

or

Serve sautéed stalks with shredded leaves in a cheese sauce (p. 126) and bake in 350°F. oven 40 minutes.

CHARD AU GRATIN / *serves 6*

3 pounds Swiss chard 2 teaspoons salt 3 tablespoons butter or margarine 3 tablespoons flour 3/4 cup milk 1/2 cup diced processed cheese	*Wash chard, cut out heavy ribs and cut into 1-inch pieces. Cook in small amount of boiling salted water for 5 minutes. Shred leaves, add to ribs and cook 5 minutes longer, drain and press out excess liquid. Make a cheese sauce (p. 126) with remaining ingredients and pour over chard in a 2-quart casserole. Bake in a 325°F. oven 45 minutes.*

CHARD AND GREEN ONIONS / *serves 6*

4 slices of bacon 2 pounds chard 1/2 teaspoon salt 1 bunch green onions, cut into 1-inch lengths 1 hard-cooked egg, sieved	*Fry bacon in skillet, remove, drain, and keep warm. Wash chard, cut away heavy ribs, and shred leaves. Put in skillet with bacon fat. Add salt and onions. Cover and cook slowly until tender. Put in serving dish; crumble bacon and sieved egg over top.*

CHARD SWISS STYLE / *serves 8*

1/4 cup milk
2 slices of bread
1/3 cup dried mushrooms
2 leeks
3 tablespoons chopped parsley and
    chives
1/2 cup chopped celery leaves
1/2 clove of garlic
4 cups cooked chopped chard
    greens
1/3 cup grated Swiss cheese
    salt, pepper, and nutmeg
4 chives
1/2 cup fine breadcrumbs
	Break the bread into small bits and pour the cold milk over it. Let stand until the milk is absorbed. Soak the mushrooms in a little warm water, squeeze dry, and chop very fine. Clean the leeks and chop very fine. Add the mushrooms, leeks, parsley, celery leaves, and mashed garlic to the bread and mix the whole with the chard greens. Add the cheese. Season to taste with salt, pepper and nutmeg. Add the unbeaten eggs, one at a time, beating well after each addition. Grease a baking dish thoroughly and turn in the chard mixture. Spread the crumbs over the top and dot with butter or margarine. Bake in 350°F. oven 30 minutes or until firm and well browned.

Tomatoes

Tomatoes are perhaps the most popular vegetable with home gardeners. The harvest period extends over several weeks and tomatoes have a multitude of table uses.

Growing Tomatoes

Do not apply too much nitrogen fertilizer to the soil in which tomatoes are grown, unless it is recommended locally.

UNSTAKED TOMATOES

Spacing	Amount	Planting dates
• rows: 3 feet apart • plants: 3 feet apart • depth: 1/2 inch	• per person: 30 feet of row, 1/2 packet of seeds • per 100 feet of row: 2 packets of seeds	• indoor: March 15 - April 15 • transplanting dates: May 24 - June 1 (or after last frost) • outdoor: after May 20 • Seedlings emerge in 7 - 12 days • Yield in 62 - 66 days • Expected crop: 400 pounds per 100 feet of row

Two plantings per season are possible.

STAKED TOMATOES

Spacing	Amount	Planting dates
• rows: 2 feet apart • plants: 2 feet apart • depth: 1/2 inch	• per person: 5 feet of row, 1/4 packet of seeds • per 100 feet of row: 1 packet of seeds	• indoor: March 15 - April 15 • transplanting dates: May 24 - June 1 • Seedlings emerge in 7 - 12 days • Yield in 75 - 82 days • Expected crop: 400 pounds per 100 feet of row

Only one planting per season is possible.

Growing Subarctic Types of Tomatoes

The subarctic tomatoes can be sown directly into the garden once the soil has warmed to above 50 degrees. When short rows are sown, the tomatoes should be planted in relays in case the first sowing is frozen by a late frost.

Spacing	Planting dates
• rows: 2 feet apart • plants: 1 inch apart (thin later) • depth: 1/2 - 1 inch	• outdoor: May 7 - May 14

TRANSPLANTED UNSTAKED

With subarctic-types from seeding to transplanting there is a wait of 5 weeks at Edmonton, Alberta, and 4 weeks at Toronto, Ontario (as examples).

Spacing	Amount	Planting dates
• rows: 3 feet apart • plants: 3 feet apart • depth: 1/2 inch	• per person: 30 feet of row, 1/2 packet of seeds • per 100 feet of row: 2 packets of seeds	• indoor: March 15 - April 15 • transplanting dates: May 24 - June 3 • Yield in 62 - 66 days • Expected crop: 400 pounds per 100 feet of row

TRANSPLANTED STAKED

Follow directions for transplanted unstaked, except that the rows are two feet apart, and the plants are grown on stakes.

Cooking Tomatoes
1 small fresh tomato (3-2/3 ounces) = 22 calories

BASIC PREPARATION

Wash tomatoes, and cut out stems. If desired, peel by dipping in boiling water for 1/2 minute, then into cold water. The skin can then be removed easily.

To fry
Slice tomatoes, and fry in a little hot fat. A pinch of sugar as well as seasoning improves the flavour.

To grill
Cut tomatoes in half crosswise, top with a little butter and seasoning. Grill steadily under moderate heat.

To bake
Halve the tomatoes, top with a little butter and seasonings and bake for 15 minutes in a moderately hot oven.

There are many fillings for baked whole tomatoes. The centre pulp is taken out, usually mixed with minced meat, creamed fish, cheese and crumbs, etc. Before filling and returning to the oven, season the tomato case well.

TOMATOES PROVENÇAL

Cut ripe, firm tomatoes in half across.
Sauté tomatoes, cut side down, in oil,
until the cut side is delicately carmelized.
Season to taste.

CHILLED BEEFSTEAK TOMATOES AND ONIONS/serves 6

2 large beefsteak tomatoes cut
    into 1/2-inch slices
1 sweet onion, sliced
1/4 cup olive or salad oil
2 teaspoons oregano
3/4 teaspoon salt

Place tomatoes and onions in alternate layers in large bowl. Mix remaining ingredients and pour over vegetables. Refrigerate one or more hours.

RICE-STUFFED TOMATOES/serves 6

6 firm ripe tomatoes
2 cups cooked rice
2 tablespoons olive or salad oil
    salt, pepper and thyme
2 tablespoons chopped chives
1/4 cup buttered breadcrumbs
    cheese sauce (p. 126)

Cut tops off tomatoes. Scoop out and chop the pulp. Sauté cooked rice in oil 5 minutes. Season with salt, pepper, thyme and chopped chives. Add tomato pulp and stuff into scooped-out tomatoes. Place filled tomatoes in a greased casserole, cut side up. Sprinkle with buttered crumbs. Bake in 400°F. oven 20 minutes. Serve with cheese sauce.

STUFFED TOMATOES/serves 4

4 large tomatoes
1 cup diced celery
1 - 2 tablespoons minced chives
2 teaspoons minced fresh dill
    or 1/2 teaspoon dried or same
    quantity sweet basil
3/4 cup mayonnaise
    lettuce

Cut top off tomatoes and scoop out pulp and seeds. Mix pulp and a small amount of juice with celery, chives or scallions and dill or basil. Stir in 1/2 cup mayonnaise. If too thick add a little tomato juice. Adjust seasoning, adding salt, pepper or lemon juice to taste. Refill tomatoes with mixture. Chill and serve on lettuce leaves topping each tomato with a generous dab of mayonnaise.

STUFFED TOMATO SALAD/serves 6

6 tomatoes
1-1/2 cups shredded pineapple
1/2 cup chopped roasted peanuts
2 tablespoons French dressing
    (p. 131)
3/4 teaspoon salt
    lettuce

Peel the tomatoes and cut slice from top. Remove seeds and pulp. Chill the tomatoes. Combine tomato pulp, pineapple, peanuts, dressing and salt. Fill tomatoes with mixture and serve on lettuce leaves.

TOMATO SALAD/serves 8

4 large tomatoes
1 teaspoon thyme
1/2 teaspoon salt
1/4 teaspoon sugar
1/2 teaspoon pepper
1-1/2 tablespoons olive oil
2 tablespoons minced chives

Peel and slice the tomatoes and arrange them in overlapping rows around a serving dish. Sprinkle with thyme, salt, sugar and olive oil, and let stand for an hour or two. Add the chives or scallions if you wish.

TOMATO AND AVOCADO SALAD/serves 6

3 tomatoes, peeled, cut in
  wedges
1 large avocado, peeled, sliced
1/2 cup French dressing (p. 131)
1 head lettuce
3 tablespoons grated cheese

Marinate the tomatoes and avocado in the French dressing in the refrigerator. Tear the lettuce into bite-size pieces into salad bowl. Add marinated tomatoes and avocado. Sprinkle with cheese and toss lightly.

BASIC TOMATO ASPIC/serves 6 - 8

3-1/2 tablespoons gelatin
3 cups tomato juice
1 cup consommé
1/4 cup sugar
1/3 teaspoon salt
2 tablespoons vinegar

Sprinkle the gelatin on 1 cup of the cold tomato juice. Heat the remaining 2 cups tomato juice with the consommé, sugar, salt, and vinegar, and pour onto the gelatin. Stir to dissolve. Pour into a large mold or 6 to 8 individual cups. Chill until set.

HERBED TOMATO ASPIC/serves 8

1/4 cup chopped celery
1/4 cup chopped onion
3/4 teaspoon salt
1/8 teaspoon freshly ground pepper
1 tablespoon sugar
1/3 teaspoon basil
1 tablespoon vinegar
1 bay leaf, crushed
2 cups tomato juice
2 tablespoons gelatin
3/4 cup mayonnaise

Cook celery and onion with seasonings in tomato juice until they are very soft. Strain. Mix gelatin in 1/2 cup cold water and add to the hot tomato mixture. Stir to dissolve. Pour into a ring mold and chill until set. Fill centre with seafood or other salad and serve with mayonnaise.

Watercress

Few indeed are the home gardeners who can provide the conditions necessary to grow this vegetable. When you know where to look, cress is found growing in natural stream beds in great abundance.

Growing Watercress

Watercress is not classified as a home garden vegetable.

Cooking Watercress
3-1/2 ounces = 19 calories

BASIC PREPARATION

Wash thoroughly in several changes of water to remove all traces of sand. Remove all tough stems and wilted portions. Cook briefly in boiling water.

To store
Wash well, shake water from the leaves and refrigerate in a tightly covered jar to keep up to 7 days.

WATERCRESS SANDWICH FILLING

Mix cooked meat with chopped watercress and celery. Moisten with mayonnaise or salad dressing.

CREAM OF CORN AND CRESS SOUP

1 small onion, chopped
3 tablespoons butter or margarine
1-1/2 cups cut fresh corn
1-1/2 teaspoons shortening
1/2 teaspoon sugar
1 cup water
1-1/2 cups milk
1/8 teaspoon pepper
1 cup chopped watercress
2 egg yolks, beaten
1/2 cup light cream
paprika

Sauté onion in butter 2 - 3 minutes. Add next four ingredients; bring to boil and simmer, covered, 10 minutes. Add next three ingredients and cook 2 - 3 minutes longer. Force mixture through a food mill or purée in a blender. Add egg yolks and cream and heat gently. Do not allow to boil. Serve with a sprinkling of paprika.

ORANGE AND WATERCRESS SALAD/serves 6

4 oranges
1 stalk celery
1/4 teaspoon sugar
1/4 cup Lemon French dressing (p. 131)
1 bunch watercress

Peel and section the oranges and shred the celery. Add sugar to the Lemon French Dressing. Pour over a mixture of the orange and celery. Pile this on watercress which has been put into a salad bowl.

WATERCRESS STUFFING/makes 3 cups

2 tablespoons chopped onion
4 tablespoons chopped celery
6 tablespoons butter
3/4 teaspoon salt
1/8 teaspoon pepper
1-1/2 cups finely cut watercress
3 cups fine, dry breadcrumbs

Cook onion and celery for 2 minutes in 1/2 of the butter. Add salt, pepper and watercress. Cook until liquid evaporates. Add remaining butter after melting to breadcrumbs and combine ingredients.

CRESS AND MUSHROOM SOUP/serves 4

1 onion, chopped
1/4 cup butter or margarine
1-1/2 cups sliced mushrooms
1-1/2 teaspoons fat
1/2 teaspoon sugar
1 cup water
1-1/2 cups milk
1/8 teaspoon pepper
1 cup chopped watercress
2 egg yolks, beaten
1/2 cup light cream
paprika

Sauté onion in butter in saucepan for 2-3 minutes. Add mushrooms, fat, sugar and water. Bring to a boil and simmer, covered, for about 10 minutes. Add milk, pepper and cress. Cook for 2 or 3 minutes longer. Purée mixture. Add egg yolks and cream; heat gently. Sprinkle with paprika.

Yams

The yam is a thick tuber which develops at the base of the plant's stem. There are more than 150 species of this root. In the raw form they are rather bitter. Some grow up to 100 pounds, and some are no larger than a small potato. The texture varies greatly.

Growing Yams

Yams require more frost-free growing days than our less-than-moderate climate permits.

Cooking Yams
3 -1/2 ounces, raw = 101 calories

BASIC PREPARATION

Peel and wash yams, then slice or cube. Cook in any way potatoes are cooked.

Yams may be used in soup; they can be mashed like potatoes; or they can be mashed and then fried or baked. They can also be boiled or baked in their jackets, or cooked with meat in stews, or sliced and fried.

The yam and the sweet potato are not the same. They resemble each other closely in taste, but belong to different plant families. But for cooking purposes, yams and sweet potatoes are interchangeable in every way.

BAKED YAMS/serves 6

6 whole yams butter salt pepper	Wash the outside of the yams well. Prick and bake for approximately 35 minutes for each pound, in a 400°F. oven. When cooked, remove the top skin, lift out the pulp, and mash with butter and seasoning. Return to shell.

ORANGE YAMS/serves 6

6 medium yams, cooked, peeled, mashed, hot 1/4 cup firmly packed brown sugar 2 tablespoons butter or margarine grated rind 1 orange 1/4 cup fresh orange juice 1/2 teaspoon salt 1/8 teaspoon pepper	Blend all ingredients; beat until light and fluffy. Put in shallow casserole and brown lightly under broiler.

ISLAND YAM AND CHEESE CRULLERS/makes 4 dozen

2 cups grated peeled yams 1/2 cup sifted flour 2 tablespoons cooking oil 3/4 teaspoon salt 1/4 cup grated Cheddar cheese 1 egg, well beaten 3 tablespoons milk fat or oil for deep frying.	Combine all ingredients except fat. Beat until well blended. Drop mixture by teaspoonfuls into deep fat (375°F.) and fry. Serve with guava jelly.

FRENCH STYLE YAMS/serves 6

1/2 cup brown sugar 2 pounds yams, peeled, cooked, cut into 6 pieces 1/2 teaspoon salt 1/2 cup dry sherry 3 tablespoons butter or margarine	Place half sugar in bottom of greased 1-1/2-quart casserole; cover with yams then remaining ingredients. Bake uncovered in 350°F. oven 30 minutes. Baste while cooking.

Final Touches

Sauces

Sauces Thickened with Flour

The sauces most commonly served with meat, fish, and vegetables consist essentially of a liquid, fat, flour, and seasonings. Because sauces are made so frequently, it is worth while to memorize the general proportions of these ingredients:

GENERAL PROPORTIONS FOR SAUCES

FAT	FLOUR	LIQUID	SALT
Butter or drippings	All purpose or pastry	milk water stock tomato juice	
2 tablespoons	1-1/2 to 2 tablespoons	1 cup	1/2 tsp

STEPS IN MAKING SAUCES

1. Melt the fat in a saucepan or the top of a double boiler. Stir in the flour.
2. Remove from direct heat and pour in the liquid. Cold liquids may be added all at once. Hot liquids must be stirred in gradually.
3. Return to direct heat and stir slowly but steadily until the sauce boils. Season to taste.
4. If the sauce is not to be served immediately, set the saucepan over hot water and cover it tightly so that a crust will not form on the surface. Otherwise, the crust will give the sauce a lumpy appearance when it is stirred into the liquid beneath.

MEDIUM WHITE SAUCE/for creamed and scalloped dishes

2 tablespoons butter
1-1/2 to 2 tablespoons flour
pepper, celery salt, or
other seasoning
1 cup milk
1/2 teaspoon salt

Follow the steps for sauces thickened with flour.

THIN WHITE SAUCE/for cream toast, cream soups

1 tablespoon butter
1 tablespoon flour
1 cup milk
1/2 teaspoon salt
pepper or other seasoning

Follow the steps for sauces thickened with flour.

EASY CHEESE SAUCE

Place 1 cup of undiluted evaporated milk in the top of a double boiler. Add 2 to 4 ounces (1/2 to 1 cup) of cheese cut into small pieces. Cook over water until the cheese has just melted. Stir until well blended and smooth. Season with salt and paprika.

CHEESE SAUCE

Add 1/4 to 1/2 cup (1 to 2 ounces) of cut or grated cheese to 1 cup of Thin White Sauce. Stir over hot water until the cheese has melted. American, Swiss, or Edam cheese may be used.

Sauces for Vegetables

ORANGE-FLAVOURED HOLLANDAISE /serves 6

1 orange
3 egg yolks
1 lemon
1/4 teaspoon salt
1 cup butter or margarine

Grate the rind of the orange into saucepan. Add egg yolks and heat vigorously until yolks are thick and sticky. Squeeze juices of orange and lemon into bowl. Beat 2 tablespoons into the yolks along with the 1/4 teaspoon salt. Place over moderate heat and beat with wire whip until mixture becomes creamy and coats the wires. Do not heat the yolks too quickly. Remove from heat, beat in the butter by drops at first (until sauce is very thick), then by teaspoons. Thin if necessary, with drops of orange and lemon juice. Taste for seasoning. Keep over lukewarm water until ready to use. Serve with asparagus or broccoli.

QUICK MIX HOLLANDAISE /makes approx. 3/4 cup

2 egg yolks
1 tablespoon fresh lemon juice
1/4 teaspoon salt
1/8 teaspoon pepper
1/2 cup butter

Combine egg yolks, lemon juice, salt and pepper in blender. Heat butter until bubbly. Slowly add butter to eggs in blender until thick.

ASPARAGUS SAUCE SALSA VERDE /makes 3/4 cup

3 tablespoons cider vinegar
1/2 cup olive oil
3/4 teaspoon prepared mustard
3 tablespoons minced finely
    chopped parsley
    watercress
1 onion, minced

Combine all ingredients and blend thoroughly.

POLONAISE /makes 3/4 cup

1/4 cup butter
1/2 cup fresh breadcrumbs
1 hard-cooked egg, finely chopped
1 tablespoon chopped parsley

Brown breadcrumbs in melted butter. Add egg and heat thoroughly. Sprinkle with parsley. Spoon over cooked drained asparagus.

GREEK EGG AND LEMON SAUCE /makes 1-1/2 cups

3 egg yolks
1 whole egg
4 tablespoons fresh lemon juice
1 cup hot chicken bouillon

Gradually beat egg yolks and whole egg until light. Add lemon juice, beating constantly. Add hot bouillon, a little at a time, beating constantly.

SAUCE RÉMOULADE/makes 2 cups

3 hard-cooked egg yolks
1/2 teaspoon salt
1/8 teaspoon pepper
1/2 teaspoon dry mustard
1 cup salad or olive oil
2 tablespoons vinegar (or more to taste)
1 onion, minced
few parsley sprigs, chopped

1 tablespoon each of minced chervil, gherkins and caper (optional)

Force egg yolks through a fine sieve. Blend with salt, pepper, and mustard. Gradually beat in oil, a few drops at a time, until all is added. Add remaining ingredients and beat well.

Sauces Based on White Stock

WHITE STOCK/makes 8 cups—partially jellied

6 pounds veal bones and meat
or
6 pounds chicken backs, necks and gizzards
or
6 pounds (altogether) veal and chicken bones and meat
1/2 cup each of sliced carrot, onion and celery
1 chopped onion
1 teaspoon salt

Bouquet garni:
1 bay leaf, 4 parsley branches, 1 thyme sprig OR 1/4 teaspoon ground thyme, and 1 whole clove, tied together.

Separate meat and bones into pieces and put them in a large pot with vegetables, salt, and herbs. Cover with water and bring to a boil. Skim off all the scum that rises to the top until all the meat has fallen from the bones and the flavour has gone into the stock. Skim occasionally during cooking. Strain, cool, then refrigerate. Next day discard the fat that has hardened on top.

SAUCE SUPREME/makes 2-1/4 cups

4 tablespoons butter or margarine
2 tablespoons flour
1 cup white stock (see above)
1 small onion stuck with 1 whole clove
1/2 bay leaf
1/4 cup heavy cream
1 tablespoon fresh lemon juice

Melt 3 tablespoons of butter and stir in flour. Gradually stir in stock. Add onion with clove and the bay leaf. Cook over low heat, stirring constantly, until smooth and thickened.

Simmer for 10 minutes. Strain. Stir in remaining butter and cream. Beat in lemon juice if desired.

Serve hot over cooked vegetables or as a base for meat and vegetable casserole.

SAUCE VELOUTÉ/makes 8 cups

This sauce isn't quite as simple to make, as you need white stock as the base. However, a large batch can be made at one time and frozen in one-cup jars.

3/4 cup butter or margarine
3/4 cup flour
8 cups white stock (see above)
1 small onion
2 whole cloves
1/2 bay leaf

Make a roux with the butter and flour. Add white stock, the onion stuck with the cloves, and the bay leaf. Bring to a boil, simmer for one hour, skimming if necessary, cool. Use as directed, or freeze for future use.

SAUCE ALLEMANDE/makes about 2 cups
For hot hors-d'oeuvre, and dishes topped with crumbs.

1-1/2 cups Sauce Velouté (see above)
2 egg yolks
1/2 cup heavy cream
salt, white pepper
fresh lemon juice

Heat Sauce Velouté until just simmering. Beat egg yolks and cream until blended. Gradually beat in a few drops at a time, 1/2 cup of the hot sauce. Add remaining sauce in a thin stream, beating constantly. Put mixture back in saucepan. Place over medium heat and bring to a boil. Cook, stirring, for 1 minute. Strain through a fine sieve. Add seasonings and lemon juice to taste. Reheat if necessary.

Note
When serving the sauce on fish, 1 - 2 tablespoons soft butter may be added, bit by bit, to finished sauce.

Salad Dressings

SAUCE VINAIGRETTE/makes 1/2 cup, enough for salad for 6
French dressing for green salads and salad combinations

1 to 2 tablespoons wine vinegar,
      or a combination of
      vinegar and lemon juice
  1/8 teaspoon salt
  1/4 teaspoon dry mustard
6 to 8 tablespoons olive or salad oil
  1/4 teaspoon pepper
  1/4 teaspoon dried herbs such
      as tarragon or basil

Beat vinegar, salt and mustard in a bowl until dissolved. Beat in the oil. Season with the pepper and herbs. Place all ingredients in a screw-top jar and shake vigorously for 30 seconds to blend thoroughly. Taste carefully for seasoning.

COCKTAIL DIP OR SALAD DRESSING

1 8-ounce carton plain yogurt
1 tablespoon dried onion slices
1 teaspoon salt
  dash pepper

Mix all ingredients together in a bowl. Leave in a cool place for 6 hours. Serve with plain cocktail biscuits, potato crisps or as a low calorie dressing for salads.

ECONOMICAL SALAD DRESSING

3/4 cup condensed milk
1/2 teaspoon salt
1/2 cup vinegar
  1 teaspoon dry mustard

Mix all ingredients, beat well. Chill before serving.

SLIMMING SALAD DRESSING

If you are a "mayonnaise lover," you can make a good substitute by blending a little seasoning and lemon juice with plain yogurt or milk.

FRENCH DRESSING/makes 2 cups

1/2 cup vinegar
1-1/2 cups olive or salad oil
1-1/2 teaspoon salt
1/4 teaspoon pepper
1 teaspoon powdered mustard
1/8 teaspoon cayenne

Mix all ingredients in a quart glass jar. Cover tightly and shake until thoroughly blended. Store in refrigerator.

LEMON FRENCH DRESSING

Substitute 1/2 cup fresh lemon juice for vinegar in French dressing recipe above.

GARLIC FRENCH DRESSING

Add 1 peeled garlic clove to French dressing.

SWEETENED FRENCH DRESSING

Add 2 teaspoons sugar to French dressing.

COTTAGE CHEESE FRENCH DRESSING
For fruit, greens, and vegetables

To 3/4 cup French dressing, add 2 tablespoons cottage cheese, 1 tablespoon pickle relish, and 2 tablespoons chopped parsley.

SNAPPY CHEESE DRESSING

4 ounces cottage cheese
2 ounces blue cheese, crumbled
1 teaspoon grated onion
1 teaspoon prepared mustard
1/2 teaspoon Worcestershire sauce
3 tablespoons fresh cream

Blend cheeses well together. Add onion, mustard and Worcestershire sauce. Fold in the cream.

CHIFFONADE DRESSING/makes 1-3/4 cups
For mixed green or vegetable salads

3/4 cup French dressing
  1 tablespoon minced parsley
  2 tablespoons chopped pimiento
  2 tablespoons chopped green
    pepper

1 teaspoon minced onion
1 hard-cooked egg, chopped

Combine all ingredients and mix well.

MUSTARD DRESSING/for rice, potatoes, or other vegetables

Blend 2 tablespoons dry mustard with enough water to make a thick paste. Dilute slightly with wine vinegar. Add salad oil and beat until creamy. While beating, add sugar and salt to taste.

HERB DRESSING/for greens, seafood, or meat

To 3/4 cup French dressing, add 2 teaspoons chopped fresh dill, marjoram, rosemary, summer savory, or other herbs.

SOY SAUCE DRESSING/makes 1 cup/For coleslaw

    2 tablespoons soy sauce
1-1/2 tablespoons water
  1/2 cup salad oil
    1 tablespoon catsup
  1/2 teaspoon minced garlic
  1/4 cup wine vinegar
    1 tablespoon brown sugar

1/2 teaspoon paprika
1/4 teaspoon pepper
  2 dashes Tabasco

Mix all ingredients.

THOUSAND ISLAND DRESSING/makes 2 cups
For greens, hard-cooked eggs or vegetables

  1 cup mayonnaise
1/2 cup chili sauce
  2 tablespoons minced green
    peppers
  3 tablespoons chopped stuffed
    olives

1 minced pimiento
1 teaspoon grated onion or
  2 teaspoons chopped chives

Mix all ingredients together.

RUSSIAN DRESSING/makes 3/4 cup/For greens

1/2 cup mayonnaise
1/4 cup chili sauce
  2 tablespoons pickle relish
  2 tablespoons red caviar (if desired)

Mix all ingredients together.

LOUIS DRESSING/makes 2 cups

1 cup mayonnaise
1/2 cup chili sauce
1/4 cup French dressing, made with
    tarragon vinegar
2 tablespoons chopped green olives
1 teaspoon Worcestershire sauce
1 teaspoon horseradish

salt, pepper
1/4 cup chopped green onions
2 tablespoons sweet pickle relish
    juice of 1/4 lemon or lime

Mix all ingredients together.

VINAIGRETTE DRESSING

2 tablespoons vinegar (wine, cider
    or tarragon)
5 tablespoons olive or salad oil
1/4 teaspoon salt
1/8 teaspoon pepper

Mix all ingredients in a bowl.

BASIC VINAIGRETTE SAUCE/makes 2/3 cup

1/2 cup olive or salad oil
3 tablespoons vinegar
    salt, pepper

Combine oil and vinegar, and beat until
well blended. Season to taste with salt
and pepper

Mayonnaises

CLASSIC MAYONNAISE/makes 1-1/2 cups

1 egg yolk
1/4 teaspoon EACH salt, pepper, and
mustard
1 cup olive or salad oil
1 tablespoon vinegar
1 tablespoon warm water

Put the egg yolk and seasonings into a bowl. Gradually beat in oil, drop by drop, stirring all the time until the mixture is thick (too much will make the mixture curdle). Beat in the vinegar gradually, then add the warm water.

CURRY MAYONNAISE/makes 1 cup

Add 1 - 3 teaspoons curry powder to 1 cup mayonnaise.

MUSTARD MAYONNAISE/makes 1 cup

2 teaspoons powdered mustard
1 tablespoon malt vinegar
1 teaspoon sugar
1 cup mayonnaise

Mix all ingredients.

CREAMY MAYONNAISE-ROQUEFORT DRESSING/makes 1-1/4 cups
For greens or vegetable salads

1/2 cup Roquefort cheese, crumbled
1 3-ounce package cream cheese
1/2 cup heavy cream
1/2 cup mayonnaise
1 tablespoon fresh lemon juice
1 tablespoon wine vinegar

Blend Roquefort and soft cream cheese. Beat in cream. When blended, stir in mayonnaise, lemon juice and vinegar.

MAYONNAISE ROUGE/makes 1 cup

To 1 cup mayonnaise, add the mashed coral from 1 cooked lobster.

MAYONNAISE WITHOUT EGGS

  1 teaspoon dry mustard
1/2 teaspoon salt
  1 teaspoon sugar
1/8 teaspoon pepper
3/4 cup evaporated milk
  1 cup olive or salad oil
  3 tablespoons wine vinegar

Put the mustard into a bowl with sugar, salt, and a large pinch of pepper. Add evaporated milk. Mix in oil slowly and beat well. When mixture thickens add vinegar. Season to taste.

FAMILY MAYONNAISE

  3 tablespoons flour
  1 teaspoon dry mustard
    few grains cayenne or pepper
1/2 teaspoon salt
  1 egg
  1 cup water
  4 tablespoons vinegar
  3 tablespoons olive or salad oil
  1 tablespoon sugar

Blend flour, mustard, seasoning and egg to make a paste. Gradually stir in the water. Add vinegar and cook over boiling water until thick. Cook for an additional 5 minutes. Cool and beat in the oil.

Vegetable Garnishes

Garnishes are edible ornaments, which are added to a prepared dish to enhance its appearance.

BEETS

CUPS
Cook medium-size beets (or rutabagas) and peel. With a sharp knife trim out the centre leaving a 1/2-inch shell. Fill as desired.

ROSES
Parboil large beets for 10 minutes, or until the skins slip off. Cool. With sharp knife cut petal-shaped scallops around lower end of beet; turn point of knife down and in. Cut around beet, removing 1/4 inch from sides above petals. Start from a point 1/4 inch above and midway between 2 petals of first row, cut down and in until knife touches tops of first row of petals. Continue around to form second row of petals. Cut around beet, removing 1/4 inch from sides above second row of petals, as in first row of petals. Continue making rows of petals until rose is complete, making 4 or 5 rows of petals, depending on the size of the beet.

CARROTS

BALLS
Cut small balls of cooked carrot with a melon baller. Use remainder of carrot for mashing.

CUPS
Cut large carrots into 1-1/2 inch pieces. Cook until tender, and carefully scoop out pulp and fill with sauce or vegetables.

CURLS
Use large fat carrots to make these. They should be fresh and at room temperature. Peel carrot, then cut off a lengthwise slice that is a quarter to half an inch thick at the top. This gives a broad, flat surface with a generous showing of lighter-coloured core. Using a vegetable peeler, cut thin strips from the flat surface, starting at the tip end. Strips sometimes curl themselves; if not, curl around finger and fasten with a toothpick. Drop into cold water and refrigerate for several hours, or put in bowl of ice water for one hour before serving.

FLOWERS
Cut scraped raw carrots into thin crosswise slices. Cut V-shaped notches into the edge of the slice. Crisp in ice water.

LATTICE
Cut lattice slices of raw carrot with a fluting knife. Cut the carrot and then turn it halfway round and make a second cut. Cut thinly to achieve an open lattice. Simmer gently and handle carefully. Can be used raw as well.

CELERY

CURLS
Cut celery into 1-1/2 inch lengths. With a sharp knife cut one end of the piece of celery into thin slices. Place in ice water to crisp and curl. Scallions may be cut in the same way.

ROSES
Fill celery stalks with softened cream cheese or an herb blend of cheeses. Put filled celery stalks back together. Tie with string and chill. Cut celery crosswise into half-inch slices and serve.

CUCUMBERS

BOATS
Cut a peeled or unpeeled cucumber in half lengthwise. Scoop out pulp leaving a 1/2-inch thick shell to be filled with any mixture desired.

CHAINS
Cut thin slices of unpeeled cucumbers. Cut a small round out of centre to form a ring. Cut each ring from one outside edge to the centre and link cucumber slices together to form a chain.

FLOWERS
Cut off ends of an unpeeled cucumber. Cut cucumber into 2-inch pieces. On each piece scoop out pulp. Cut peel partially to form 5 petals. Place in ice water to curl peel into petals. Fill centre with a carrot slice or shredded carrots.

FLUTED SLICES
Run the tines of a fork down the length of the cucumber so that the entire surface is scored. Cut into thin slices and crisp in ice water. This can be done with peeled and unpeeled cucumbers.

TWISTS
Cut thin slices of unpeeled cucumber. Cut each slice from one outside edge to the centre. Pull the cut pieces in opposite directions to form an S-shape twist. Hold in place with toothpick and chill in ice water.

ONIONS

CHRYSANTHEMUMS
Peel a medium-size red onion. Cut onion into thin slivers from the pointed end down, leaving the bottom attached. Place in ice water to crisp and flare the petals.

CUPS
Cook whole, large peeled onions until tender but still firm. Scoop out centre pulp leaving a half-inch shell. Fill as desired.

RINGS
Peel onion and cut into thin slices. Separate into rings and use raw or dip into batter and fry.

POTATOES

BALLS
Cut balls of raw peeled potato and simmer carefully in salted water until tender.

BASKETS
Baskets can vary in size from very small to large. Shred raw potatoes and wash well in cold water. Place shreds in a layer in a sieve. Press another sieve into the first sieve. Lower into deep fat or oil and fry until crisp. Remove from oil and carefully pull out basket. Drain on absorbent paper. Fill as desired.

LATTICE
See Carrot Lattice; potatoes are usually deep fried.

MASHED
Use a large star-tipped pastry bag filled with mashed cooked sweet or white potatoes to decorate planked dishes, to shape duchess potatoes, and to fill orange cups. Potatoes can be scooped out of their shells after baking, mixed with seasonings, and restuffed.

STICKS
Cut peeled potatoes into long thin matchstick pieces and deep fry until brown and crisp.

RADISHES

CRISSCROSS
Make parallel cuts from tip of stem of fat squat radish. Give radish a quarter turn, make second set of cuts. Put in bowl of ice and water.

FAN
Make thin parallel cuts, not quite to stem end, on long oval radish. Let stand for about 30 minutes at room temperature. Spread fanlike. Crisp in ice water before serving.

ROSE

Use firm, oval-shaped radishes of a good size. Using a sharp knife with a thin point, thinly slice the outer red skin into petals. Place in ice water and the petals will fan out during chilling. The white inside part of the radish may be cut flat and a coil of pimiento strips used for the inside of the rose.

TULIP

Make cuts through peel only from tip to stem around radish. Cut peeling back to make petals. Put in bowl of ice and water.

TOMATOES

CUPS

Make zigzag diagonal half-inch cuts into the side of the tomato all the way around the centre of the tomato. Pull apart. May be used as is or scooped out and filled. Cut off a thin slice from top and scoop out pulp for a larger and deeper tomato cup. It may be necessary to remove a thin slice from the bottom to keep tomato steady on the plate, or cut tomato, peeled or unpeeled, into wedges, leaving them jointed at the bottom. Spread open and fill as desired.

ROSE

Cut the peel from a large tomato in one long strip, having the strip about 1-inch wide. Coil the strip into a tight roll, keeping the bottom part a little tighter than the top part. Use parsley sprigs or other green leaves to decorate rose.

To make a Tomato Cheese Rose, whip cream cheese. Wash and dry small tomatoes. Fill a teaspoon with the cream cheese and level it off with a knife. To form cheese petals, hold the filled teaspoon against the side of the tomato. Press the cheese on the tomato with a downward stroke of the spoon. Place sieved egg yolk in the centre of the flower. Chill before serving. Petals can be shaped around the tomato, repeating the process for a second and third tier of petals.

OTHER VEGETABLE GARNISHES

BOUQUET

Cut off one-third of a grapefruit. From remaining piece scoop out about half of centre. Tie parsley together to make a tight bouquet to fit into grapefruit. Stick strong toothpicks into bottoms of beet roses and radish flowers and arrange on parsley. Add other garnishes.

DAISIES

With sharp knife tip, cut out V-shaped sections from edge of slice of carrot, rutabaga, or cucumber. Put a small round of contrasting colour in centre, for example, a ripe olive or a grape.

PICKLE FANS

Thinly slice a medium-sized sweet pickle lengthwise to within 3/4 inch of end. Spread to form fan.

SLICED VEGETABLES

Thinly slice one-inch pieces of carrot, cucumber, or whole radishes to within 1/8 inch of opposite side. Put in ice water for several hours to open.

Nutrition Chart

Name		Description	Serving Size (Volume)	Weight	Calories	Protein gm.	Fat gm.	Carbohydrate gm.	Calcium gm.	Sodium mg.	Iron mg.	Vitamin A i.u.	Thiamine mg.	Riboflavin mg.	Niacin mg.	Vitamin C mg.	Food Exchanges
Artichokes	Fresh	3" dia.	—	—	33	1.5	.2	6.0	.024	22.0	1.0	180	.80	—	—	6.0	1 group A vegetable
Asparagus	Fresh	Green	1/2 c. or 6 spears	—	18	1.6	.2	2.9	.016	—	.7	750	.12	.14	1.08	25.0	1 group B vegetable
Beans-green	Fresh	Fresh	1/2 c.	2 oz.	14	.9	.1	3.0	.023	—	.5	330	.05	.60	.30	9.0	1 group B vegetable
-Lima	Fresh	cooked	1/2 c.	2-1/2 oz.	76	4.0	.3	15.0	.023	—	1.3	230	.11	.70	.90	12.0	1 bread
-wax	Fresh	cooked	1/2 c.	2 oz.	14	.9	.1	3.0	.023	—	.5	330	.05	.60	.30	9.0	1 group B vegetable
Beets	Fresh	cooked	1/2 c.	3-1/2 oz.	34	.8	.1	8.1	.017	110.0	.6	15	.01	.03	.20	5.0	a group A vegetable
Broccoli	Fresh	cooked	1c.	5 oz.	44	5.0	.3	8.2	.195	26.0	2.0	5100	.10	.22	1.2	111.0	
Brussel Sprouts	Fresh		1c.	4-1/2 oz.	60	5.7	.6	11.6	.044	15.0	1.7	520	.05	.16	.60	61.0	
Cabbage	White	cooked	1 c.	5 oz.	40	2.4	.3	9.0	.078	8.5	.8	150	.08	.08	.50	53.0	1 group A vegetable
		raw	1c.	3-1/2 oz.	24	1.4	.2	5.3	.046	5.0	.5	80	.06	.05	.30	50.0	

Name	Form	Description	Serving Size (Volume)	Weight	Calories	Protein gm.	Fat gm.	Carbohydrate gm.	Calcium mg.	Sodium mg.	Iron mg.	Vitamin A i.u.	Thiamine mg.	Riboflavin mg.	Niacin mg.	Vitamin C mg.	Food Exchanges
Carrots	Fresh	cooked	1 c.	5 oz.	44	.9	.7	9.3	.038	34.0	.9	18130	.07	.07	.70	6.0	1 group A vegetable
	Raw	grated	1 c.	4 oz.	45	1.3	.3	10.2	.043	34.0	.9	13200	.06	.06	.70	7.0	
Cauliflower	Fresh	cooked	1 c.	4 oz.	30	2.9	.2	5.9	.026	—	1.3	108	.07	.10	.60	34.0	1 group B vegetable
		raw	1 c.	3-1/2 oz.	25	2.4	.2	4.9	.022	22.0	1.1	90	.11	.10	.60	69.0	
Celery	Fresh	cooked	1/2 c.	2 oz.	12	.8	.1	2.2	.030	—	.3	—	.03	.02	.20	4.0	1 group B vegetable
		raw	1/2 c.	2 oz.	12	.8	.1	2.2	—	55.0	—	600	.02	.06	.20	5.0	
Chicory	Fresh	raw	1/4 small head	1/2 oz.	3	.2	.1	.4	.016	—	.1	1429	.01	.03	—	2.0	free food
Chives	Fresh	chopped	1 tbsp.	1/4 oz.	4	.3	.1	.6	.004	—	.6	38	.01	—	—	6.0	free food
Corn	Fresh		1 ear 5" x 1-3/4"		84	2.7	.7	20.0	.005	—	.6	390	.11	.10	140	8.0	1-1/2 bread
Cucumber	Raw	peeled	7-1/2" x 2"	1-1/2 oz.	25	1.4	.2	5.5	.020	.9	.6	—	.07	.09	.40	17.0	1 group B vegetable
	Raw		6 slices	2/3 oz.	6	.4	—	1.4	.005	.9	.2	—	.02	.02	.10	4.0	
Eggplant	Raw		2 slices-1/2 c.	8-1/3 oz.	60	2.8	.5	13.7	.037	2.3	1.0	7.5	.10	.12	120	13.0	1 bread
Endive	Raw		1/2 lb. or 9 small leaves		45	2.7	.5	9.1	.179	81.0	.39	6800	.15	.27	.99	25.0	
Fennel	Leaves	raw	1/2 lb.		58	—	—	—	—	—	—	—	—	—	—	—	
Kale	Fresh	cooked	1 c.	3-1/2 oz.	45	4.3	.7	7.9	.248	7.0	2.4	9220	.08	.25	1.90	56.0	1 group A vegetable
		raw	1" 3 c.	6 oz.	77	6.8	1.0	12.6	.394	194	3.8	13220	1.8	4.60	3.50	201.0	
Kohlrabi	Raw	cooked	1 c.	5 oz.	47	3.3	.2	10.4	.071	—	.9	—	.06	.06	.30	57.0	
		diced	1 c.	4-1/2 oz.	41	2.9	.1	9.2	.063	—	—	—	.08	.07	.30	84.0	
Leeks	Raw	raw		1/2 lb.	62	—	—	—	—	—	—	—	—	—	—	—	

Name	Description	Description	Serving Size (Volume)	Weight	Calories	Protein gm.	Fat gm.	Carbohydrate gm.	Calcium gm.	Sodium gm.	Iron mg.	Vitamin A i.u.	Thiamine mg.	Riboflavin mg.	Niacin mg.	Vitamin C mg.	Food Exchanges
Lettuce inc. Iceberg & Boston	Raw	raw	2 large or 4 small leaves / 1-2/3 oz.	7	.6	.1	1.4	.011	6.0	.2	.2	270	.02	.04	10	4.0	1 group B vegetable
Mushrooms		diced	1/2 c. / 1-2/3 oz.	8	1.2	.1	2.0	.005	2.5		.5	—	.05	.22	2.50	2.5	free food
Mustard greens		cooked	1 c. / 4-2/3 oz.	31	3.2	.4	5.6	.308	68.0		4.1	10050	.08	.25	1.00	63.0	1 group A vegetable
Okra	Raw		8 oz.	70	—	—	—	—	1.0		—	—	—	—	—	—	
Onions	Cooking	raw	2-1/2" dia. / 3-2/3 oz.	49	1.5	.2	11.3	.035	1.0		.6	60	.04	.04	.20	10.0	1 group A vegetable
			1 tbsp. / 1/3 oz.	4	.1	—	1.0	.003	—		—	—	—	—	—	1.0	
Onions	Cooked		1 c. / 7 oz.	79	2.1	.4	18.3	.067	—		1.0	110	.04	.06	.40	13.0	1 bread
Parsley	Raw	chopped	1 tbsp. / 1/10 oz.	1	.1	—	.3	—	—		.2	290	.01	.01	.10	7.0	free food
Pimiento			1 medium / 1 oz.	10	.3	.2	2.2	.003	—		6	870	.02	.02	.10	36.0	free food
Potatoes white		baked	1 medium	97	2.4	.1	22.3	.013	—		.8	20	.11	.05	1.40	17.0	2 group A vegetables
	Boiled	peeled	1 c. / 4 oz.	105	2.5	.1	24.1	.014	.8		.9	20	.12	.04	1.30	17.0	
	Boiled	unpeeled	1 medium / 2-1/2" dia. / 5 oz.	118	2.8	.1	27.1	.016	—		1.0	30	.14	.06	1.60	22.0	
Radishes	Fresh		4 small or 3 medium / 1/3 oz.	4	.2	.02	.8	.008	3.0		.15	4	.02	.01	.25	3.0	1/2 group B vegetable
Rutabagas		cooked cubed	1 c. / 5 oz.	50	1.2	.2	11.6	.085	—		.6	540	.08	.11	1.10	330	
	Raw	diced	3/4 c. / 4 oz.	45	1.3	.1	10.5	.066	6.0		.5	396	.08	.09	1.10	43.0	
Parsnips	Raw	cooked	1 c. / 5 oz.	94	1.6	.8	21.5	.088	—		1.1	—	.09	.16	.30	19.0	2 bread
		diced	2/3 c. / 4 oz.	94	2.1	1.3	33.0	.036	8.5		.8	—	.16	.14	.20	21.0	

145

Name		Description	Serving Size (Volume)	Weight	Calories	Protein gm.	Fat gm.	Carbohydrate gm.	Calcium gm.	Sodium mg.	Iron mg.	Vitamin A i.u.	Thiamine mg.	Riboflavin mg.	Niacin mg.	Vitamin C mg.	Food Exchanges
Peas	Fresh	raw	1/2 c.	2-1/2 oz.	74	5.0	.3	13.3	.016	—	1.4	510	.26	.12	2.00	20.0	1 group A vegetable
		cooked	1 c.	5 oz.	111	7.8	.6	19.4	.035	—	3.0	1150	.40	.22	3.70	24.0	
Peppers	Green	cooked		2 oz.	17	.8	.1	3.9	.007	—	.3	480	.03	.05	.30	64.0	1 group B vegetable
	Raw		1 medium	2 oz.	16	.8	.1	3.6	.007	.8	.3	400	.02	.04	.20	77.0	1 group B vegetable
Spinach		boiled	1 c.	2-2/3 oz.	46	5.6	1.1	6.5	—	—	3.6	21200	.14	.36	1.10	54.0	1 group A vegetable
	Raw		1/2 c.	4 oz.	22	2.6	.3	3.6	—	82.0	3.4	10680	.13	.23	.70	67.0	1 group B vegetable
Squash	Summer	cooked	1 c.	7 oz.	34	1.3	.2	8.2	.032	—	.8	550	.08	.15	1.30	23.0	1 group A vegetable
		raw diced	1-1/3 c.	8-1/3 oz.	40	1.5	2.5	9.8	.038	—	1.0	650	.12	.22	2.00	51.0	
Squash	Winter	baked & mashed	1/2 c.	3-1/2 oz.	46	1.9	.4	11.3	.025	.3	.8	6345	.05	.15	.60	7.0	
		boiled & mashed	1/2 c.	4 oz.	43	1.7	.4	10.0	.022	—	.7	5645	.05	.12	.50	6.0	1 group A vegetable
		raw & diced	1-1/2 c.	8-1/3 oz.	95	4.5	.7	22.0	.049	.7	1.5	12375	.12	.30	1.20	20.0	1 bread +
Swiss Chard	Fresh leaves	cooked	1 c.	6 oz.	47	46	.7	8.4	—	—	4.4	16960	.07	.28	.50	30.0	1 group A vegetable
	Fresh	raw	1-1/2 c.	3-1/2 oz.	24	1.4	.2	4.4	.105	84.0	2.9	3220	.07	.08	.50	44.0	1 group B vegetable
	Leaves & stock	cooked	1 c.	5oz.	30	2.0	.3	6.4	.152	—	3.6	4510	.06	.09	.60	25.0	1 group A vegetable
Tomatoes	Fresh		1 small (1-3/4" x 2-1/4")	3-2/3 oz.	22	1.1	.3	4.4	.012	3.0	.7	1210	.06	.05	.60	26.0	1 group B vegetable
Turnip greens	Fresh	cooked	1 c.	5 oz.	43	4.2	.6	7.8	.376	—	3.5	15370	.09	.59	1.00	87.0	1 group B vegetable
		raw	1/2 c.	1-2/3 oz.	15	1.5	.2	2.7	.129	5.0	1.2	4770	.05	.23	.40	78.0	

Metric Conversions

The following charts and lists represent a guide only. There is no direct conversion for recipes, only some general rules and guidelines.

Metric Symbols to Remember

Quantity	Name of Unit	Symbol
Temperature	degree Celsius	°C
Volume	litre	ℓ
	millilitre	ml
Mass	gram	g
	kilogram	kg
Length	metre	m
	centimetre	cm
Energy	joule	J

LIQUID MEASURE

Liquid measure cup = 250 ml which is graduated in 25 ml divisions.

DRY MEASURE

These measures are available in units of three: 250 ml, 125 ml, 50 ml. Conversion to metric usually involves a 5 per cent increase in amounts. All ingredients should be rounded up or down to the nearest unit.
Small liquid and dry measures are available in sets of five: 1 ml, 2 ml, 5 ml, 15 ml, 25 ml. The 25 ml is similar to a typical coffee measure. All ingredients should be rounded to the nearest measure.

MASS (WEIGHT)

You will need to know these units when shopping for meats, fruits, and vegetables.

1 kilogram (kg) = 1000 grams = a little more than 2 pounds.

Examples:	1 slice of bread	= approx.	25 g
	1 boiled egg	= approx.	50 g
	1 apple	= approx.	150 g
	1 orange	= approx.	175 g

LENGTH

The centimetre (cm) slightly less than 1/2 inch will be a common unit for measure. In pan sizes, thickness of meat, rolled doughs, distance from broiling unit or distance between cookie sheets.

Examples: 1 six-inch rule   = 15 centimetres
           width of little finger   = 1 cm
           8″ x 8″ cake pan   = 20 cm square cake pan
           Shortbreads   = 1cm thick
           Ranges   = 75 cm wide (30″)
           Steak for barbecue   = 4 cm thick (1 3/4″)
           Meat balls   = 3 cm in diameter

TEMPERATURE – CELSIUS SCALE

Freezing point of water 0°C   32°F.
Boiling point of water 100°C   212°F.

A Guide to new temperature:

230°F.	=	110°C
250°F.	=	121°C
270°F.	=	132°C
300°F.	=	149°C
325°F.	=	160°C
350°F.	=	175°C
375°F.	=	190°C
425°F.	=	220°C
450°F.	=	230°C

When baking in an ovenproof glassware pan reduce temperature 10°C.

     Refrigerature Temperature = 4°C
     Freezer Temperature   = −18°C

Here is a sample recipe converted to metric measures.

TUNA, PEAS AND RICE/serves 6

REGULAR STYLE MEASURE	*METRIC MEASURE*
1 onion, chopped	*1 onion*
3 tablespoons butter or margarine	*75 ml*
3 cups cooked peas, hot	*750 ml*
3 cups cooked rice, hot	*750 ml*
1 7-ounce can tuna	*250 ml*
1-1/2 teaspoons salt	*5 ml*
1/4 teaspoon pepper	*1 ml*
1/4 cup grated Parmesan cheese	*25 ml*

Sauté onion in butter until golden; add to next five ingredients. Heat and serve with cheese.

Index of Recipes

Growing instructions for each vegetable are found on pages listed as the major reference for the vegetable.

77 01790 110 70